The Mini

Vincent F. Hendricks
Camilla Mehlsen

The Ministry of Truth

BigTech's Influence on Facts, Feelings and Fictions

Translation by Andre Amtoft &
Anja Amtoft

Copy-editing by Vincent F. Hendricks

 Springer

Vincent F. Hendricks
Center for Information and
Bubble Studies
University of Copenhagen
Copenhagen, Denmark

Camilla Mehlsen
Mehlsen Media
Copenhagen, Denmark

ISBN 978-3-030-98628-5   ISBN 978-3-030-98629-2   (eBook)
https://doi.org/10.1007/978-3-030-98629-2

Cover image: Chie Hidaka via Getty Images.

This Springer imprint is published by the registered company Springer Nature
Switzerland AG
The registered company address is: Gewerbestrasse 11, 6330 Cham, Switzerland

To Elon, Jack, Jeff, Mark, Shou, Sundar, Susan, Tim …

Prologue

BigTech, Big Problems

The advent of a new decade was indeed *some* dawn for digitalized society as a whole and BigTech in particular. Front and center, disruptions and disturbances as tangible as theoretically tricky, materialized for people, politicians, and police to immediately see and literally feel in the flesh.

A new chapter in the American history was written when hundreds of demonstrators stormed the US Congress bearing weapons, bulletproof vests, and various MAGA—*Make America Great Again*—merchandise. As members of the Senate and House gathered to formalize Joe Biden as the official winner of the US Presidential election 2020, would-be insurrectionists in Washington D.C. shouted "Stop the steal!" outside in concert with a trending hashtag #stopthesteal online. Shortly before, outgoing President Donald J. Trump had held a long speech for the dissenters in a park across from the White House. In his speech, Trump falsely claimed that his election defeat was due to massive election fraud—now known as #thebiglie—and went on to encourage his followers to march down Pennsylvania Avenue to Congress and overturn the election as "you will never take back our country with weakness."[1] The Capitol siege on January 6th, 2021, marked the most severe attack against an American official institution in over 200 years.

The following day, the actions of a small group of tech executives initiated what has since become known as "Deplatforming Day": Facebook, now Meta,[2] put a cork in Donald J. Trump's Facebook and Instagram profiles "indefinitely and for at least the next 2 weeks until the peaceful transfer of power is complete", as posted by founder and CEO Mark Zuckerberg in his own Facebook profile on January 7th, 2021. Twitter's co-founder and chief officer, Jack Dorsey, went further and permanently shut down Donald J. Trump's account, noting that the president had conspired to incite violence and social unrest and would continue to do so.

Google and Apple removed the Parler app from their Play and App stores because Parler failed to intervene when Trump supporters used the app to incite violence. Google subsidiary YouTube banned channels with Trump-related video content that spread misinformation. TikTok removed videos promoting the Capitol siege, Reddit banned the "r/DonaldTrump" group for inciting violence and threats, and Snapchat permanently erased Trump's account the day he left the Oval Office, January 20th, 2021.

---

[1] Haberman, M. (2021). "Trump Told Crowd 'You Will Never Take Back Our Country With Weakness'", *New York Times*, 06.01.2021, verified 11.01.2022: https://www.nytimes.com/2021/01/06/us/politics/trump-speech-capitol.html.

[2] In October 2021, Facebook changed its name to *Meta* at the Facebook Connect augmented and virtual reality conference reflecting the fact that the company's ambition goes way beyond just being social media consisting of services like Facebook, Instagram, and WhatsApp—it is a universe with omnipresent aspirations. In the current text, Meta/Facebook are used interchangeably and sometimes in conjunction depending on the context but signify the same company entity.

Deplatforming Day marked a milestone for social platforms and BigTech (i.e., tech platforms that have secured market dominance through the attention economic business model, see Chap. 2). Blocking a US President's profile is a powerful signal that what happens on online platforms has off-line consequences. It simultaneously suggests that platforms have begun to edit more heavy-handedly in order to live up to the social responsibility that they—like it or not—have for the substantive and sprawling digital democratic infrastructure they run and manage. Deplatforming Day was a demonstration of the power platforms wield over public space, debate, and democracy. The public sphere where opinions are expressed and democracy lives is now, in no small measure, on private digital hands and subject to what resembles a monopolized power structure.

By their sheer size, vast reach, and fine print guidelines, social platforms and tech services possess the ability to shape our understanding of facts and fictions, amplify our feelings—whether it be anger or joy—and initiate mass mobilization. Societal citizens are now to a large extent also users of the Internet. Facebook, with its 2.9 billion users, is the world's largest social platform, while Facebook-owned services WhatsApp, Messenger, and Instagram have another 2 billion, 1.3 billion, and 1.4 billion users, respectively. YouTube has almost 2.3 billion users and TikTok 1 million users.[3] These social platforms not only have more users than the number of people that the Human Rights Commission in the Hague refers to and protects on a daily basis, but also command a vastly outsized content portfolio compared to the Hague or any other supranational organization, all the way up to the UN.

---

[3] Most popular social networks worldwide as of October 2021, ranked by the number of active users, verified 27.01.2022: https://www.statista.com/statistics/272014/global-social-networks-ranked-by-number-of-users/

But who decides where the line should be drawn for what can or cannot be published online and for what should receive attention? What do social platforms do with videos that show the burning of the Quran, peddlers of holocaust denial, hate speech, or racist rhetoric? And what about deep fakes of politicians as porn stars or in heavily intoxicated performances? Or live transmissions of mass murder, decapitation, suicide, substance abuse, self-harm, or hunger strike? What do social platforms do about anti-vaxxer groups, flat-earthers, and conspiracy theorists? And how about bare breasts, "dick pics," or sexualized G-string content? What responsibility do we as a society have when a platform such as TikTok creates editorial guidelines whose aim is to demote content and views from so-called ugly, poor, and old users?[4]

It sounds conspicuously like issues and problems pulled out of George Orwell's dystopian novel *1984*. In 2021, the *Wall Street Journal* started publishing an investigation which almost read like a chapter out of *1984*.

In September 2021, the *Wall Street Journal* began reporting on irregularities and inconsistencies in the administration of user profile privileges on Facebook stemming from leaks of classified internal documents provided by a whistleblower known as "Sean." In October 2021, "Sean" came forward and identified herself as Frances Haugen, a former product manager in Meta/Facebook's civic integrity team.

In what came to be known as the *Facebook Files*, which Haugen leaked, showed that the company, among other things, had a program running called XCheck providing a VIP list consisting of approximately 5.8 million profiles made up of celebrities, politicians, and other high-profile users, enjoying particular privileges as they do not have to live up to the Facebook community standards to the same

---

[4] Bidle S. et al. (2020). "Invisible Censorship", *The Intercept*, 16.03.2020.

degree as more regular users.[5] The VIP profiles have a greater freedom in what they decide to write even if what is authored is on direct collision course with the community standards. Soccer player Neymar, former president Donald J. Trump and sons, senator Elizabeth Warren, and Mark Zuckerberg himself were among the profiles being accordingly entitled.

On Facebook, we are all equal, and the rules of Facebook apply to all as Mark Zuckerberg has declared on a routine basis.[6] This brings to mind another book by Orwell—*The Animal Farm*; some are more equal than others ... when it is good for business. The leaked documents demonstrate furthermore that Facebook in an attempt to change its public image turned up the volume and number of stories in newsfeeds that reflect on the company positively but dialed down the attention to stories putting Facebook in a less flattering light.

At least as bad, but probably even worse, a later leak is witness to the fact that internal research conducted by Meta/Facebook unequivocally shows that especially youth girls and teens may suffer from low self-esteem to eating disorders by being on Instagram. It brings back memories as to how the American tobacco industry for years kept silent about the harmful consequences and hazards of smoking.[7] It was now Meta/Facebook's *tobacco moment*.

The *Facebook Files* draw a rather grim and disconcerting picture of a company riddled with flaws that cause harm, a social platform which cares little about privacy, protection of

[5] Horwitz J. et al. (2021). "The Facebook Files: A Wall Street Journal Investigation", *Wall Street Journal*, 01.10.2021, verified 11.01.2022: https://www.wsj.com/articles/the-facebook-files-11631713039

[6] Ibid. Horwitz et al. (2021): https://www.wsj.com/articles/facebook-files-xcheck-zuckerberg-elite-rules-11631541353

[7] Hilts P.J. (1994). "Tobacco Company Was Silent on Hazards", *The New York Times*, 07.05.1994, verified 11.01.2022: https://www.nytimes.com/1994/05/07/us/tobacco-company-was-silent-on-hazards.html

youth and children, propagation of misinformation and fake news, and democracy as a whole to mention but a few unnerving instalments from the files. According to the whistleblower, it is a company stoking divide, which stimulates polarization, fuels violent behavior and social unrest, fans the flame of hate speech and bullying, and lies to the public, the powers to be, and even shareholders—puts profit before most other concerns and generally has lost its moral compass if the company ever had one. A telling example is from the presidential election 2020 where Facebook took active and effective steps to block the proliferation of misinformation only to drop the efforts after the election as it was bad for engagement, traffic, data harvest, and thus profits.[8]

Many social platforms have consistently and emphatically argued and heavily lobbied for the gospel that they merely provide bandwidth, information navigation instruments, and search opportunities for their users and therefore cannot be subject to media regulations, press ethics, and press councils or even be categorized as media at all. If responsibility for content is to be placed anywhere, it is with the users. There is, however, no such thing as unrestrained freedom of expression on social platforms and search services—there never has been and probably never will be. There is quite a lot that users cannot write or publish—for both moral and legal reasons, just as specific content, standards, and guidelines across a platform are subject to continual change.

As problems ranging across nudes, self-harm content, misinformation, and terror pile up on social platforms, the boundaries are being pushed towards greater and greater editorial interference from the platforms' content moderation

---

[8] Cleave, K.v. (2021): "Internal Facebook documents detail how misinformation spreads to users", *CBS News*, 05.10.2021, verified 11.01.2022: https://www.cbsnews.com/news/facebook-whistleblower-frances-haugen-documents-misinformation-spread/

units. There is a lack of clarity as to who bears responsibility when what happens on online platforms subsequently transpires into live action off-line.

The power that social platforms exercise over the public sphere and our private lives is not merely a question of whether they ban profiles, downgrade content, or otherwise sanction online activity. Behavioral design and content moderation affect facts, feelings, behavior, and narratives on a deeper level. The force of might changes the digital and analogue worlds alike when social platforms manage virality and emotional outbursts as well as decide which formats, images, videos, words, profiles, fictions, and forecasts are given attention, toned down, or removed entirely.

When platforms tweak design functions and features, they may significantly affect the behavior of users. A small and seemingly indifferent "like" on social platforms may not seem important but, since Facebook launched the like button in 2009, it has gained colossal influence on everything from the self-esteem of youth to the spread of fake news and the election of politicians—*Do you like me? Am I good enough?*

A retweet makes it easy to share stories on Twitter and may perhaps save lives if the information circulated is about evolving earthquakes, tsunamis, virus outbreaks, and imminent unrest (or riots). However, according to Chris Wetherell, who programmed the retweet button for Twitter—and since roundly regretted doing so—the retweet incited a massive quest to go viral and quickly spread rumors and misinformation.[9]

More than 70% of the time spent watching videos on YouTube is spent watching footage that YouTube's algorithm

---

[9] Kantrowitz, A. (2019). "The Man Who Built The Retweet: 'We Handed A Loaded Weapon To 4-Year-Olds'", *Buzzfeed*, 23.07.2019, verified 31.05.2021: https://www.buzzfeednews.com/article/alexkantrowitz/how-the-retweet-ruined-the-internet

has suggested—auto-play features in recommender-based systems are efficient digital designs, the purpose of which is to provide users with customized content to get them to stay just a bit longer.[10]

In the fight against misinformation around Covid-19 and vaccines, platforms have adjusted a long list of different design features to limit the spread of misinformation and bolster the messaging of healthcare authorities and researchers. Facebook, for example, employed minor behavioral modifiers to prevent the spread of Covid-19 by using top banners to remind users to wear face masks.

Politicians have finally—clued and keyed in—come to understand the power of platforms, just as everyone was duly awakened when a president, with the biggest megaphone of all, was banned from the public sphere. However, few have dealt with the underlying mechanisms and their growing importance for democratic discourse, public space, and private life. The time is now to focus on how platforms manage attention and communication with their opaque algorithms that push content to capture and retain users—or conversely, monolithically downgrade content to prevent it from garnering attention and going viral.

The platforms' design and moderation decisions have strong bearings on which narratives are allowed to circulate and what is censored, and not least what is perceived as true or false for whom and for what. Even though BigTech routinely announce their disinterest in being arbiters of truth, it is easy in both miniscule and monumental matters to stealthily do just that with formulaic community standards, editorial guidelines, recommender-based algorithms, and behavioral design features.

---

[10] Solsman, J.E. (2018). "YouTube's AI is the puppet master over most of what you watch", *CNET*, 10.01.2018, verified 08.07.2021: https://www.cnet.com/news/youtube-ces-2018-neal-mohan/

The most important thing is not whether you as a user have a voice on social platforms but whether your voice is heard. Even though anyone with access to platforms and thus online public sphere may scream and shout from the top of their lungs, it is not the same as, nor is it a guarantee of, being heard. In the digital information structure, attention is inherently unevenly distributed—some voices are heard more often and louder, while yet others are drowned out; who receives how much attention and why and how are in large part up to the privatized tech platforms making their infrastructure and public space (un)available to users and which are therefore able to make ongoing changes to the premises of what receives attention.

It might be that users, citizens, and society at large have access to a public bullhorn, but the volume, direction, and subsequently virality of one's message are controlled and directed by someone else. It is an inherently powerful position to manage information access, the public sphere, and what should receive attention—indeed, it is every autocrat's wet dream. The power of this information control is global since the Internet is global. The rule and reign of BigTech stretch from more or less autocratic regimes to liberal democracies throughout the world. Autocratic regimes and liberal democracies usually do not agree on much, but the one thing they do agree on is that neither want a third autocratic ruler dictating what is true or false, right or wrong, valuable, beautiful, ugly, lustrous, or dull. That would file under a Ministry of Truth ….

Citizens—and the users of the Internet—must be mobilized to take active ownership and responsibility for how the digital domain develops, or else we risk ending, as George Orwell aptly describes in *1984,* with a "Ministry of Truth" rewriting facts and falsifying history to fit an overarching doctrine:

The Ministry of Peace concerns itself with war, the Ministry of Truth with lies, the Ministry of Love with torture and the Ministry of Plenty with starvation. These contradictions are not accidental, nor do they result from ordinary hypocrisy: they are deliberate exercises in *doublethink*.[11]

The platforms' management may at times consciously (or unconsciously) resemble an act of doublethink in their ability to hold two opposing opinions and beliefs at the same time: We do not want to be the arbiters of truth, but yet we pass judgement on, and decide, what (narrative) truth is by what is granted attention.

This book is to demonstrate, through various phenomena, like fake news, influencers, and nudes, that social platforms control the facts, feelings, narratives and fictions of our time in such a comprehensive manner that the platforms are *de facto* arbiters of truth. Those who control attention first control the narratives and therefore also what will be perceived as the truth. The largest social platforms and online services are reminiscent of a moralizing, normative, and behavior-modifying Ministry of Truth, whose emergence and development have consequences not only for truth, lies, and bullshit but also for our past, present, and future—and for democracy.

And in 2022, the Russian invasion of Ukraine sparked not only a veritable war in Europe, but mobilized weaponized narratives and took information warfare to new heights using in no small measure social platforms as intercontinental boards of messages. Launch tubes for everything from reliable information and eyewitness reports from the grounds of bombardment and terror to autocratic efforts of mis- and disinformation, fake news, bullshit or downright attempts to shut down news outlets, ban social platforms, cripple

---

[11] Orwell (1984): 25.

information borne infrastructure and shake up democracies at large.

With the expansion of social platforms, the digital public sphere is now in the hands of private enterprise. The platforms constitute, both a democratic infrastructure and an editorial authority determining what information enters the personal and public spheres, and not least what is given the most attention.

It might seem like it is all too little, too late—the lead of BigTech is simply too vast for society to reel in. Citizens, politicians, and legislators have been couched somewhere between the fascination of unrealized potential and naïve ignorance of all the pitfalls tech and digitalization afford. Meanwhile, BigTech have laid claim not only to just about every substantial piece of information and data, and thus our essential human values, but also to the massive economic growth of the digital attention economy.

As a global society, we could throw in the towel and wait for dystopia to materialize by itself: Humans are marionettes, and BigTech are the puppet masters. Or else, we come to realize that it is up to us to determine the path of technological development; it is we, the people, who run the show and must act and mobilize as individuals, institutionally and ideologically.

As authors, we have previously dealt with the question of individual and institutional mobilization. We have facilitated initiatives on digital education aimed at children, youth, and adults, through educational programs and presentations to students, educators, educational leaders, and parents, as well as contributed to national and international commission reports and made recommendations for politicians to enact (inter)national initiatives aimed at lifelong digital literacy for users and legislation to protect children and young people in the digital realm.

The time is ripe for a structural and systematic analysis of the biggest players of the information age of which the goal is ideological mobilization, policy-making, and realization of responsible human agency and a working deliberative democracy—not version 2.0—but a lasting version with staying power.

Vincent F. Hendricks | Camilla Mehlsen
Copenhagen | June 2022

Acknowledgments

This book has profited from the assistance of many: Our thanks go first to Andre Amtoft and Anja Amtoft in charge of translating this work from the Danish version, *Sandhedsministeriet: Techplatformenes indflydelse på tidens fakta, følelser og fortællinger* (København: Informations Forlag, 2021). They did an indeed admirable job of turning the English translation vivid and yet precise. We would secondly like to thank our Danish publisher, Informations Forlag, and the capable staff we have worked with while writing, editing, and launching the Danish version in 2021.

The research conducted for this book was only made possible by a generous grant from the Carlsberg Foundation to the Center for Information and Bubble Studies (CIBS) with the University of Copenhagen. We would in addition like to thank Dr. Mads Vestergaard, Prof. Ethan Zuckerman, and Prof. Robert C. Becker for their pointy and pertinent comments on earlier drafts of this monograph. The book references research on the impact of influencers conducted by the Media Research and Innovation Center at the University of Southern Denmark—special thanks to Prof. Arjen Van Dalen, Prof. Peter Bro, and Associate Prof. Ralf Andersson for inspiring collaboration. Thanks to Children's Welfare and the ambitious commitment to combat digital infringements and improve the digital lives of children and young people.

Finally, we would like to thank Springer Nature, including editors Christopher Coughlin, Ties Nijssen, and Floor Oosting and production manager Kritheka Elango, for standing by this project all the way and seeing it meticulously through to completion.

Contents

List of Figures

List of Tables

a Member of the Danish Ministry of Culture's Media Board as well as a Member of the Djøf Tech Commission. She is the author of several books on digital technologies and education, and her work has been published in various newspapers and magazines. She writes the Media Column for MediaWatch—a journalistic site covering the Danish media industry.

1

From Citizen to User in the Marketplace of Ideas

"I'm not a businessman, I'm a business, man."

–Jay Z

With a public bullhorn in hand and a camera firmly pointed at oneself and the outside world, every user of social platforms is virtually their own media outlet. Anyone may broadcast their lives to a potential global audience and while doing so take on the hybrid role of journalist, photographer, editor and broadcaster wrapped into one. Users may trade a myriad of information products on the marketplace of ideas. Selfies, Sudoku tips, knitting patterns, and fun memes.

But there isn't equal access for all, since the marketplace of ideas hasn't been able to muster level playing fields for the ideas, products and services that float around in what was originally intended as a free, independent and democratic cyberspace. Someone or something surreptitiously managed to put themselves in power and are now largely calling the shots.

© The Author(s), under exclusive license to Springer Nature Switzerland AG 2022
V. F. Hendricks, C. Mehlsen, *The Ministry of Truth*,
https://doi.org/10.1007/978-3-030-98629-2_1

1.1   Selfie Society

Little mirror on the wall, who's the fairest of them all?

Every day the queen asks the same question of her magical mirror and hopes the mirror will promptly answer back: "Thou, O Queen, art the fairest in the land." In the digital era we all have a magic mirror and we all compare our beauty and popularity to the rest of the kingdom subjects. Social platforms like Instagram, Facebook, TikTok, Twitter and Snapchat are types of mirrors or exchanges measuring our popularity by the numbers of 'thumbs up', hearts, followers, views, comments and other forms of 'engagement'. The big difference between the queen's magic mirror and the social platform's mirror is that in the fairytale of Snow White, it is solely the queen receiving an answer. On social platforms the answer is often freely available within the network (Mehlsen and Hendricks 2020).

Social platforms are built with functionality that make it as smooth as it is simple for users to size up each other's popularity. When we post on our profiles, payoff comes in the form of likes and comments—or angry faces, downvotes and diligent dismissals for that matter. The apparent popularity is immediate for others to see in terms of likes and followers on the *emoji exchange*, as platform algorithms reward content with many likes by featuring it as popular content to other users.

Within the past few years there has been a substantial surge in people's communication about themselves online. It is not unusual that technological innovations create new norms for human interaction and communication. In 1450, Gutenberg's printing press was a groundbreaking invention that made mass production of books viable and helped spread information and knowledge around. But this change happened over several decades. What is new now, is the speed by which technological innovation forges new communicative norms and fundamentally changes conditions for people as for society.

The selfie, for instance, has installed a new communicative norm that has taken us by storm. A decade ago it seemed way too vain to take pictures of yourself in public and flash it to friends and acquaintances from near and far—"look at me!". Today taking and sharing selfies with the outside world is not only about as normal as it can possibly be to drink tea. It also signals a fundamental change in social interaction over a very short period that notably coincides with the successful merger of smartphones and social platforms to create an optimal framework for disseminating selfies. In hindsight, and to put things into perspective, it was only in 2013, that the word "selfie" entered our colloquial vocabulary and became the *Oxford Dictionary* word of the year.

It was also in 2013, that the Prime Minister of Denmark then, Helle Thorning-Schmidt, took a selfie with heads of state, former US-President Barack Obama and former UK-Prime Minister David Cameron, during the memorial service of Nelson Mandela in South Africa. The press, heavily present at the event, captured the minor off-script scene and images of the three smiling heads of state went viral and circulated in newspapers around the globe. Thorning's selfie received criticism on several accounts for being as inappropriate as it was considered tasteless considering the circumstances of memorial service. It didn't help that first lady Michelle Obama appeared unamused in some of the footage that captured the moment (Fig. 1.1).

It wasn't until 2017 Helle Thorning-Schmidt revealed her selfie to the world. *The Washington Post* named Helle Thorning-Schmidt's selfie the seventh best political photo of 2013; *The New York Times* called her selfie a democratization

Fig. 1.1 Helle Thorning-Schmidt possibly took her first selfie, with Prime Minister David Cameron and President Barack Obama—and Michelle Obama on the sideline—during the memorial service of Nelson Mandela in Johannesburg in December 2013

of image making.[1] Whether or not the selfie is in poor taste or democratizing, one thing is certain—it encapsulates a new era: the selfie-society.

Yet another famous selfie-moment occurred during the 2014 Oscars ceremony, when American host Ellen DeGeneres gathered a group of Hollywood stars to take a selfie. Immediately after, DeGeneres posted the photo on Twitter with the caption:

If only Bradley's arm was longer. Best photo ever. #oscars.

Thereby she also signaled it was American actor Bradley Cooper who took the picture with her cell phone.[2]

[1] Cilizza, C. (2013). "The 18 best political pictures of 2013", *The Washington Post*, 17.12.2013, verified 13.08.2021: http://www.washingtonpost.com/blogs/the-fix/wp/2013/12/17/the-18-best-political-pictures-of-2013

[2] Ellen DeGeneres (2014). Twitter, 03.03.2014, verified 08.07.2021: https://twitter.com/theellenshow/status/440322224407314432?lang=en

Fig. 1.2 Bradley Cooper's selfie for the Academy Awards 2014 using Ellen DeGeneres cell phone featuring among others Meryl Streep, Ellen DeGeneres, Brad Pitt, Kevin Spacey, Julia Roberts, Angelina Jolie and Lupita N'yongo

The selfie instantly went viral and remained on the top 10 list of the world's most shared tweets through the 2010s, with more than three million retweets (Fig. 1.2). *Time Magazine* wrote "It was a moment made for the celebrity-saturated Internet age" and included the Oscar-selfie on the list of 100 most influential photos—not because of the quality of the photo, but precisely because of the magnitude of its circulation (Fig. 1.3).

As *Time Magazine* noted, the Oscar-selfie illustrates that "everyone is a photographer, a publisher and a consumer".[3] It is no longer the exclusive domain of press photographers and established media outlets to snap photos and distribute them to a larger audience. Everyone may join in. Selfies also work as autographs: Instead of getting a handwritten autograph of

[3] Goldberg, B. (2016). "Most Influential Photos", *Time*, 28.11.2021, verified 01.06.2021:https://time.com/magazine/us/4574474/november-28th-2016-vol-188-no-22-23-u-s/

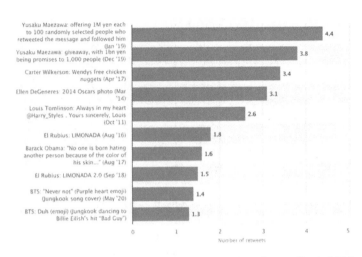

Fig. 1.3 The 10 most popular tweets on Twitter (up until July 2020, according to *Statista*). Ellen DeGeneres' tweet with the Oscar-selfie is number 4 on the list

a famous person, the new norm is to take a selfie with the famous person and share it on social platforms.

In 1964, Canadian media theorist Marshall McLuhan proclaimed *the medium is the message.* With this famous line he conceived that a given medium influences the surrounding society and literally creates new types of environments. With cell phones in pocket and profiles on social media platforms we have stepped into an age where we might add: *Man is the medium* (Mehlsen 2020a). YouTube encapsulates this very idea in its slogan: "Broadcast Yourself," or as Instagram notes, "Capture and Share the World's Moments". There is no longer an editor to prevent you from going live or being broadcast, as long as you remain within the bounds of the official and ever changing platform's community standards or guidelines. To be one's own medium is thoroughly a form of strategic communication, where users become homespun marketing consultants that speculate in virality—*What will get the most attention? A selfie, a sunset or bare skin?*

The explosion of selfies is possibly a function of the many likes these posts tend to get on social platforms. In pursuit of the perfect selfie, the least lucky have tragically lost their lives (so-called "selfiecides") typically by drowning, falling from a high place, getting run over, shooting oneself by mistake or being attacked by an animal. Between 2011 and 2017 a total of 259 people died while taking selfies versus the 50 souls killed by sharks.[4]

The selfie is a measurable product in the digital information market, where attention is the desired return. On social platforms, users of all ages, shapes and sizes share selfies to get a response. There is the 'duckface', also known as pouty lips, which accentuates the cheek bones, the 'fish gabe' with slightly open lips so the teeth barely show and send a seductive signal, or the completely natural smile #withoutfilter. Like fashion phenomena, the standards for selfies develop over time and become markers in different cultures and subcultures.

Regardless of culture, the premise is the same: A selfie is a unit the value of which may be negotiated and exchanged by users—and that has caught the eye of politicians. If politicians share a political message, for example on Instagram, the selfie is an investment object, that brings added attention to their message—a selfie in exchange for the attention of potential voters; a personal, spontaneous, direct, unfiltered and authentic "digital handshake" between politicians and their constituents.

Former president Barack Obama may have considered Ellen DeGeneres's Oscar selfie as a "cheap stunt" but was caught in the very same act with heads of state Helle

---

[4] Keeley, N. (2019). "More People Die Taking Selfies Than by Shark Attacks" *Newsweek*, 29.06.2019, verified, 01.06.2021: https://www.newsweek.com/selfies-deadlier-shark-attacks-1446363

Thorning-Schmidt and David Cameron a year before.[5] Former president Bill Clinton posted a selfie with Microsoft founder Bill Gates in 2013 with the caption: "Two Bills, one selfie." As of January 2022 one may on gettyimages.com leisurely choose from a stockpile of almost 600 different Trump selfies in "Premium, High Res Photos".[6] Presidents, congressmen, governors and aspiring politicians have all figured out what it is with selfies—it is about political capital in the attention economy as Erik Smith, working on Obama's presidential campaigns, have pointedly formulated it:

> In a world where politicians are often packaged and marketed and kind of touting a brand, the authentic things get a lot more attention.[7]

Social platforms use algorithmic architectures that rank information according to what is most popular among the users in the network. All of this information, including your online identity, belongs to the platforms. Your profile, for example, on Snapchat, Facebook, Instagram, TikTok or Twitter is not *yours*: "Your" profile belongs to the provider of the social platform. The provider owns your entire digital identity: texts, photos, likes, social network data, interaction patterns, engagement records etc. It is also the provider who decides which template you present yourself in, and in the final analysis, what you're allowed to present, how you present it, and not least, for whom. They provide server space and direct traffic on their social platforms. Social platforms

[5] Kopan, T. (2014). "Obama: Ellen selfie 'cheap stunt'", *Politico*, 20.03.2014, verified 04.01.2022: https://www.politico.com/story/2014/03/obama-ellen-selfie-104846

[6] "589 Donald Trump Selfie High Res Photos", verified 04.01.2022: https://www.gettyimages.dk/photos/donald-trump-selfie

[7] Villacorta, N. (2014). "The politics of the selfie", *Politico*, 21.03.2014, verified 04.01.2022: https://www.politico.com/story/2014/03/selfies-politics-104910

thereby mimic a form of brokerage firm deciding how information products are displayed, exchanged and sold. In the attention economy, platforms play the part that banks and financial institutions play in the money economy. If a sale is successful in terms of return likes, comments and 'upvotes' the social platform is sure to harvest its own return in engagement, traffic and useful data dividends when profiles and selfies repeatedly shine in the light of attention.

With the rise of 'selfie society', everybody is their own media outlet. The word "citizen" now incorporates the digital users and consumers of the Internet and other actors of the information marketplace. Anyone can take a selfie, broadcast their own world for public consumption and gain access to the marketplace of ideas. But is this access equally distributed among users, consumers and citizens?

1.2   Markets for New Truths

On October 23, 2019 Facebook's founder and director, Mark Zuckerberg, testified in front of the American Congress' Financial Service Committee to report on *Libra*. *Libra* is Facebook's blueprint for creating a digital currency—a testimony to Facebook's ambitions to conduct something reminiscent of banking. Before Zuckerberg was finished speaking, he was questioned, or nearly grilled, by democratic congresswoman Alexandria Ocasio-Cortez. In their exchange Zuckerberg admitted that misinformation campaigns may be bought on Facebook, largely independent of whom the buyer in the end turns out to be. Zuckerberg also stated that Facebook will not take editorial responsibility, even if what is being advertised is indeed false.

- **Alexandria Ocasio-Cortez:** "Do you see a potential problem here with a complete lack of fact-checking on political advertisements?"
- **Mark Zuckerberg:** "Well, Congresswoman, I think lying is bad, and I think if you were to run an ad that had a lie in it, that would be bad. That's different from it being, in our position, the right thing to do to prevent your constituents or people in an election from seeing that you had lied."

Zuckerberg's response created considerable debate pertaining to the editorial responsibilities of social platforms. It also reinforced the perception of many that the social platforms massively prioritize profit over all other considerations and with a high risk of misinformation as a result. You may purchase and disseminate fake news on Facebook, if you can afford it. These—and other—serious suspicions and appalling allegations pertaining to profits before people attitude of the company on multiple counts, were dramatically reinforced by former Facebook/Meta employee, now turned whistleblower, Frances Haugen's, extensive leaks of internal Facebook documents now known as the *The Facebook Files* originally published in the *Wall Street Journal* in 2021 (Fig. 1.4).[8]

After the insurrection on Capitol Hill in Washington DC on January 6, 2021, Zuckerberg changed course with Facebook suspending outgoing president Donald J. Trump's accounts on Facebook and Instagram. Zuckerberg proclaimed on his Facebook profile on January 7, 2021, that the president was a danger:

> We believe the risks of allowing the President to continue to use our service during this period are simply too great.

---

[8] Horwitz, J. et al. (2021). "The Facebook Files: A Wall Street Journal Investigation", *Wall Street Journal*, 01.10.2021, verified 04.01.2022: https://www.wsj.com/articles/the-facebook-files-11631713039

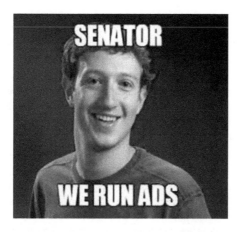

Fig. 1.4 A widely shared meme highlighting Republican senator Orrin Hatch's ignorance of the social platform's business model under a senate hearing with Mark Zuckerberg in 2018—in the aftermath of the Cambridge Analytica Scandal. Orrin Hatch asked how Facebook can maintain a business model where users don't pay for Facebook's service. Mark Zuckerberg, with a suppressed smirk, replies with a brief answer, "Senator, we run ads"

> Therefore, we are extending the block we have placed on his Facebook and Instagram accounts indefinitely and for at least the next 2 weeks until the peaceful transition of power is complete.[9]

A long list of other social media platforms also closed Donald J. Trump's account or removed misinformation related to Donald J. Trump, including allegations of election fraud and #StoptheSteal-campaign online during the 2020 American presidential election. This deplatforming of Donald J. Trump is evidence to the effect that social platforms are starting to edit content in a more deliberate and aggressive manner with reference to the social responsibility that they *de facto* have

---

[9] Zuckerberg, M. (2021). Facebook, verified 08.07.2021: https://www.facebook.com/zuck/posts/10112681480907401

"The shocking events of the last 24 hours clearly demonstrate that President Donald Trump intends to use his remaining time in office to undermine the peaceful and lawful transition of power to his elected successor, Joe Biden.

His decision to use his platform to condone rather than condemn the actions of his supporters at the Capitol building has rightly disturbed people in the US and around the world. We removed these statements yesterday because we judged that their effect -- and likely their intent -- would be to provoke further violence. (…)

Over the last several years, we have allowed President Trump to use our platform consistent with our own rules, at times removing content or labeling his posts when they violate our policies. We did this because we believe that the public has a right to the broadest possible access to political speech, even controversial speech. But the current context is now fundamentally different, involving use of our platform to incite violent insurrection against a democratically elected government."

Fig. 1.5 Facebook pulls the plug on Trump. Mark Zuckerberg's post on his Facebook profile January 7, 2021

given the extensive (democratic) infrastructure they both have created and daily administer (Fig. 1.5).

Difficult dilemmas exist for Zuckerberg & co.—and many other social media platforms and BigTech companies. On the one hand, they don't want to assess and decide who gets to have a public voice and who doesn't, just as they don't want to decide what can, should and may be said. On the other hand they retain the right to boot people, fakes and stories off their platform as they see fit relative to their community standards, editorial guidelines or self-appointed content moderator units such as Facebook's Content Oversight Committee, where the aforementioned Helle Thorning-Schmidt among others sits at the table.

A market for new truths, however, has emerged with social platforms. A market where platforms decide whether a conspiracy theory, a political meme or one of the many other information products should be allowed on the platform. Yet still, the platforms do not want, as Zuckerberg has repeatedly stated, to be *arbiters of truth*. But that was in effect the cards they were dealt when they co-opted the digital marketplace of ideas.

1.3   The New Marketplace of Ideas

The digital revolution was supposed to bring emancipation. In the *Declaration of the Independence of Cyberspace* from 1996, the American essayist and cyberlibertarian activist John Perry Barlow (1947–2018) declared the new digital reality, *cyberspace*, a brand new and independent world of freedom and equality, that supersedes the Old World Order with states, governments and their accompanying levers of control and repression. Barlow compares the digital revolution to the American Revolutionary War and the digital pioneers to the heroes of the American Revolution. Cyberspace is freedom from suppression, freedom to move around freely and to think freely—on the Internet we are free among and with each other's exchanges, relationships, thoughts and ideas.[10]

The highly resilient notion that a free and unfettered communication and exchange of ideas is an emancipatory and desirable act, is however, not new. The English philosopher and political economist John Stuart Mill (1806–1873), in his masterwork *On Liberty* from 1859, compared the freedom to express and develop ideas, with the structure and dynamics of a free financial market. Here, consumers dictate the level of demand for any given product on the market while producers and retailers are in charge of supply. Given the preferences and limited resources of consumer's, the law of supply and demand will sooner or later inadvertently

---

[10] John P. Barlow (1996): *Declaration of the Independence of Cyberspace*, verified 14.01.2021: https://www.eff.org/cyberspace-independence

determine the value of the goods on the market. The value of the item is determined by the degree with which it is accepted by the consumers. The free market is a system where the price of goods and services is self-regulated and determined by the right of buyers and sellers to freely negotiate in an open and unregulated market.

Similarly, Mill imagined a free and open market for opinions, thoughts and ideas. A free and transparent market for public conversation plays out in parliamentary assemblies, courtrooms, the public speaker corner and in the media where all kinds of ideas are put into circulation in order to win support. The truth will thereby emerge triumphantly as that which is correct and able to win support over other competing ideas. In this process even the most imbecile and outrageous ideas are tolerated as truth will always survive in the end and falsities eventually weeded out in the liquid market of people exchanging views, opinions and ideas.

The notion of a marketplace of ideas has often been advocated as a core argument for defending free speech, a free press and liberal democracy as such. However, it was not Mill who coined the term. The term "marketplace of ideas" was first introduced by US supreme court justice William O. Douglas in his opinion in the United States vs. Rumely case of 1953. The case was about a publishers' lobby and press activities and Douglas deliberated on that:

> Like the publishers of newspapers, magazines, or books, this publisher bids for the minds of men in the market place of ideas.[11]

While Barlow in *Declaration of the Independence of Cyberspace* insists on a marketplace of free ideas as a goal, in and of itself,

---

[11] *United States v. Rumely*, 345 U.S. 41 (1953), verified 14.04.2021: https://supreme.justia.com/cases/federal/us/345/41/

Mill perceived it as a means to the truth. They were, however, both proponents of regulating markets as little as possible—thus avoiding censorship—so that all ideas, at least at their outset, share equal opportunity and that no thoughts are more privileged or able to enjoy preferential treatment by other means. In plain English this is called "level playing fields" and it expresses a situation where all enjoy and have a fair and equal chance for success with their undertaking.

Both Mill and Barlow would probably be very disappointed in the information age: It has not been able to muster level playing fields for ideas, products or services on the Internet, in general and on social platforms, in particular. Throughout decades, a hopeful narrative was spun that the Internet is a democratic construct, a means for everybody to be able to access information and have a public voice e.g. through the profiles that we as citizens and users have on social platforms.

If the marketplace for ideas and information products were free and unregulated, everything would be fine and dandy, and the attention economy would find its natural equilibrium, at least theoretically. But there is no level playing fields. The information infrastructure is privatized and social platforms do not necessarily answer to truth and democracy, supply and demand but instead to their own rules and regulations and narratives that provide companies with advertising possibilities and shareholders with dividends.

Online attention is not distributed in a way that musters level playing fields for all involved parties. In addition, it should be noted that it is private enterprise which, to a vast extent, singularly decide what type of information products are available on the marketplace and the accompanied pricing.

Arrived we have at the information age and the digital revolution. Until now we rode on the back of the

Enlightenment, where knowledge and information were conceived as the main levers to liberate peoples and stimulate the emerging democracies around Europe and the US. Information was seen as a boon not a bane. If the pioneers had been asked if public space should be allowed to be capitalized by private enterprise, their answer would have been a firm and resounding—NO! Everyone should have equal access and no one should be granted special privileges or interests in the marketplace of ideas, where democracy lives and strives on level playing fields among citizens. But that's not how the marketplace of ideas came to evolve when society's citizens became Internet users—and the products of platforms.

2

From User to Product in the Attention Economy

"It's not because anyone is evil or has bad intentions. It's because the game is getting attention at all costs."

– Tristan Harris

The tricky task right this moment is to seize your attention long enough to get you through the first few sentences, then the rest of the chapter and hopefully the whole book. Your attention is the gateway to your consciousness. The words on these pages are fighting for your attention, in tough competition with all the other interesting things happening offline as well as online at this very moment. And the social platforms are sure to remind you of all the things you're missing out on (if you haven't yet already, then just check your phone).

It pays for social platforms to speculate in what sort of information you and other users are willing to spend your limited attention on. The more information you consume online, the more attention you pay and the more engagement, traffic and data you generate. This data can then be harvested, broken down, analyzed, packaged and sold or

© The Author(s), under exclusive license to Springer Nature Switzerland AG 2022
V. F. Hendricks, C. Mehlsen, *The Ministry of Truth*,
https://doi.org/10.1007/978-3-030-98629-2_2

leased to various interested parties and advertisers. In essence, this is the business model of a legion of platforms and cadre of online services in the information market and new digital attention economy.

2.1   The New Asset: Attention

The information age holds a particular place in human history, in the sense that we have never been able to access as much information as we may now. Facebook users post 510,000 comments, create 293,000 status updates and upload 136,000 photographs every minute. On a daily basis Facebooks' 2.9 billion users share approximately 6 billion pieces of information and stream 100 million hours of video. On Twitter 6000 tweets are sent out every second, corresponding approximately to 350,000 tweets a minute. This adds up to 500 million tweets a day or almost 200 trillion tweets per year. Meanwhile YouTube excels with 500 hours of video uploaded every minute and around five billion videos shown on its platform daily (Hendricks 2021). Add to this other social platforms, such as TikTok, Snapchat, Pinterest, LinkedIn, Discord, Reddit, blogs, online-fora and encyclopedias, study portals, digitized public archives, private and covert databases, and we're confronted with head spinning amounts of data and information. Coupled with our limited time and attention we wind up with an intense supply and demand situation and a frenzied battle for our attention. Just as we can only drink a certain amount of water, there is a limit to how much information we can absorb, and absorbing it will, in any event, divert our attention from elsewhere.

In the twenty-first century, it's not microchips, windmills or solar panels, but the attention of mankind which is the new top asset. Already back in 1971 the American professor of psychology and Nobel prize laureate in economics, Herbert Simon (1916–2001), prophesied about what would become the greatest asset and most valuable resource in the information age:

> In an information-rich world, the wealth of information means a dearth of something else: a scarcity of whatever it is that information consumes. What information consumes is rather obvious: it consumes the attention of its recipients. (Simon 1971)

Attention is a scarce and valuable cognitive resource—but also a potentially highly profitable capital asset. Herbert Simons' insight is the basis on which the term "attention economy" is coined. In a market for information products ruled by an attention economy the trick is to come up with a business model in which one may profit from exchanging information for attention. This very business model is behind some of the worlds' largest corporations and has gained outsized importance not only on people's daily lives but also on the conditions for democracy in the twenty-first century.

Attention is a peculiarly elusive and fleeting type of resource in comparison to more tangible assets such as stocks, real estate, and cash money. In contrast to the latter, attention can't be:

1. neatly and equally split with one unit of attention to each recipient,
2. tossed into the air and caught (or dropped) like coins for recipients to receive,
3. collected into a pile,
4. deposited in the bank with the intent of using or withdrawing it later, and with potential added interest.

Attention is a zero-sum game when used. Paying attention to one thing, you lose out on another and we don't multitask very well although we of course often claim otherwise. The term FOMO (**F**ear **O**f **M**issing **O**ut) describes the phenomena of always having one's cell phone close at hand and constantly checking various platforms, so as not to miss out on untouched messages and other assorted information. It is integral to the business model of social platforms that users are reminded that they're *missing out* on something if they're not on the platform e.g., via color red notifications. Regardless of how long you stay, there is never enough time and attention to take it all in, but that doesn't mean you're not welcome to hang out and hang in there a little longer—the more the merrier for the social platforms.

Attention is not only a valuable cognitive resource for those from whom it is taken but likewise for those who demand it, as there is substantial value to both the paying and receiving of attention from others. The Austrian architect and economist George Franck has studied this latter part of the attention economy quite comprehensively (Franck 1999; Vestergaard 2022).

Receiving attention from others brings comfort—as a private person, syndicated business, and social platform. To be liable to attention, to be seen and heard, is both necessary for our self-esteem and for any form of communication. Being the recipient of attention may be a *goal* in itself—take fame and the prestige that comes along—just as it may be a *means* to commercial, cultural, or political influence. According to Franck, we live in a social reality comparable to a bonfire of the vanities that burns stronger and bigger as competition for attention grows fiercer by the day (Franck 2016).

Attention may function both as currency and capital, according to Franck. For attention to work as a currency the qualitative and individual value of receiving attention needs to be quantifiable. The value of a $100 bill is not tied to whom from which it is received, it is merely worth 100 dollars. For attention to play the same role in the attention economy as cash money does in the pecuniary economy, it needs to be homogenized and turned into quantitative, measurable, abstract and comparable units.

Transforming attention into countable abstract units, is made possible by channeling the information that is exchanged for attention through a *medium*. When information becomes what Franck calls *mediated information*, and when an accounting system is in place that may quantify and measure the attention invested in exchange for information, then attention works like a currency. The press and established media have long since developed and installed accounting systems to this end. Television audience trackers, newspaper readership ratings, breaking news engagement measured by the number of shares, etc., and clicks on news sites are all metrics accounting systems quantifying the amount of attention received.

Thus media institutions—syndicated as well as social platforms—may be viewed as investment bankers in the attention economy. When mass media and social platforms furnish causes or people with physical or virtual column space, entries or time on the air, they fix them up with what is akin to a form of attention credit. The media receive part of the attention that the person or cause attract from readers, listeners or viewers. The media invests in people, cases and causes by providing them with time on display and thereby the opportunity to attract yet more attention, in order to harvest additional dividends from the attention paid by their readers, listeners, viewers and users (Hendricks 2021).

2.2   Information Products

In the attention economy there is a long list of diverse information products, and more or less established common knowledge of their meaning and how much they are worth. A successful information product may be measured by the amount of attention it attracts in terms of clicks, views, emojis, comments and related posts. Selfies, videos and memes are information products, while likes/emojis, reactions, comments, and shares say something about the value of these products. For example, the number and quality of emoji-reactions say something about how much attention the market allocates to some information product and thereby signals what it is worth. Depending on whether you're the messenger, service provider or platform, it follows that the more engagement, traffic and attention you get, the more data may be harvested from followers and users. In short, there is something to be gained for all parties involved.

Like any other market, the information market may be used for a myriad of different purposes, depending on who and what your interests are. Here's a simple model for attracting attention: take a nudie in the bathtub, add a provocative caption "For a good time, call …", use the selfie in your 'story' and wait to see how your ex and the general information market react in terms of user engagement and traffic. This is pretty much what the former actress Hannah Montana, now known as pop icon Miley Cyrus, did in January 2021. In the attention economy the post was quite effective; it reached Cyrus' more than 120 million Instagram followers immediately and from there quickly spread to tabloid, lifestyle and fashion magazines and porn sites.

However, the market for such an information product is heavily regulated by the provider Instagram, as evidenced by the young star strategically covering up certain body parts in the nudie portrait. You can flash skin, but not be too naked or show female nipples (unless you're breastfeeding, have breast cancer or are a work of art) on Instagram, but genitals are an absolute no go. Such provisions must be carefully considered by the supplier if the information product is to find its way to the Instagram-regulated marketplace of images—nudes included. Once the information product has passed Instagram's community guidelines and found its way to the market, everyone can leverage their judgements or vested opinions.

In a Danish Broadcasting Company DR3 documentary, *Fie,* Danish reality star and influencer, Fie Laursen, quite precisely describes the attention economic model; how she made use of it and why she eventually decided to delete a blog she had for 10 years as well as scrub her social media profiles altogether. Deleting loads of videos on her YouTube channel, Laursen remarks there is "so much clickbait, there is [*sic*] so many commercials, there is [*sic*] so many violent video titles where I share my private life. When I see that, I know it isn't because I wanted to share. I simply did it to generate an income and keep my name in the celebrity ranks."

Fie Laursen views her blog posts and videos as investments i.e., stocks that can secure returns, for building her brand and status as an influencer. Or as she says in the documentary:

> I think what people don't understand is that when I delete 1000 YouTube videos I'm also deleting 1000 videos that provide me with an income. When I delete my blog, I'm also deleting 'affiliated links'. For me it's like having stock. Even though I've already made the video, it's still there generating money.

As an influencer Fie Laursen was snap to understand the business model of the digital attention economy: Her

YouTube content works as an investment that creates financial value down the road via the attention it generates. This is why influencers make use of methods, such as 'clickbait' and extremely private content, that work quite well in an attention economy. Thus, when Fie Laursen deletes her videos it is akin to her losing market shares.

2.3   The Attention Economy Business Model

Paying and receiving attention drives the attention economy's business model. Users, platforms and various online-service providers generate information which other users spend their attention on. Spending attention generates engagement and traffic, which in turn creates the user data that social platforms and tech-companies collect, curate, analyze, and subsequently package and sell as finely masked and segmented ad-packages to interested advertisers. It is from this simple advertisement model that the tech industry has spun its fortunes. In essence it rests on capitalizing on our attention: Our online behavior is translated into behavioral data, which in aggregated form is sold to companies for the purpose of predicting the future behavior of different segments and for mapping the potential of influencing them.

This is also known as the business model of *surveillance capitalism*, as illustrated in Fig. 2.1 (Zuboff 2019). This business model is one of the most potent and pervasive ever invented by mankind. While industrial capitalism exploits reserves of natural resources such as oil, coal, gas and the processing of raw materials, surveillance capitalism rests for its exploitation on the cognitive resources of humans. As Zuboff notes, Google was the first platform to implement the model of surveillance capitalism, even though they had

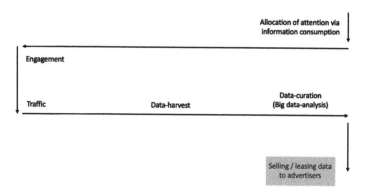

Fig. 2.1   The attention economic business model of tech platforms

declared, in the 1990s, that they would never be ad-driven. But around 2001, after the dot-com bubble burst and the ensuing economic downturn, Google began generating ad-revenue via its enormous data bank repositories of, and subsequently knowledge of, user behavior, linking them to algorithm based and automated systems that effectively targeted advertisements to users. During their 2004 stock listing, Googles' financial statement revealed that their earnings had risen by 3590% from 2001 to 2004 (Zuboff 2019a).

The data users voluntarily, involuntarily, knowingly and unknowingly provide to platforms free of charge, in exchange for attention, is what platforms profit from by renting or selling these data to third party vendors. As users we tend to think of ourselves as the consumer, but in reality we are the product itself. User profiling and predicting behavior is not only interesting for a company that has a product to sell, but also for institutions, organizations or nation states that seek to influence the behavior of its citizens e.g., stopping the spread of COVID-19 in populations or consolidating autocratic ambitions, as say in China.

Data sales are massive and concentrated on very few hands. Meta/Facebook and Google in particular have sat on more than half of all digital advertisement budgets over the past years, and are now locked in a bidding war to sweep up the remaining competition.[1]

2.4   Uneven Distribution of Attention

Now attention is both a currency and a form of capital. In terms of capital, attention holds the ability to accumulate and attract even more attention down the road. Precisely as seen in the fiduciary economy, this ability is also self-reinforcing in the attention economy. Stars and celebrities are not only famous for what they say, do or produce. They are also famous for being famous. Attention attracts attention, and attention thereby comes with interest and compound interest.

A guiding principle from the Gospel of Matthew also applies to the attention economy: Those who are already beneficiaries will benefit even more, or as expressed by Jesus in several passages in the *New Testament*, Gospel of Matthew.

> For to everyone who has, more will be given, and he will have abundance; but from him who has not, even what he has will be taken away. (Matt. 25:29)

The term "Matthew effect" was coined by sociologist Robert K. Merton who, in his groundbreaking 1968 article in *Science*, "The Matthew Effect in Science", leveraged the socio-psychological principle that even in science, success tends to breed success or put differently, advantages tend to accumulate. On a microlevel this means that the more

---

[1] Wakabayashi, D. & Hsu, T. (2021). "Behind a Secret Deal Between Google and Facebook", *The New York Times*, 17.01.2021, verified 27.01.2021: https://www.nytimes.com/2021/01/17/technology/google-facebook-ad-deal-antitrust.html

prominent researchers, independently of how much work they themselves actually put in, tend to harvest the most recognition for the output of their research group. On a macro level, the consequence is that the researchers, scientific institutions and countries that are visible and actively participate in scientific debates, gain more attention as measured by the number of citations and other bibliometric indicators. The more one has, the more one gets in return. This applies not only to science but also to a long list of other living conditions, including how attention among online agents is distributed from individual users to BigTech.

The Matthew effect is built on the principle of accumulated advantage. When a social agent, whether an individual or a group or a whole nation, gains even a small advantage over other agents, this advantage yields both interest and compound interest over time and becomes an even greater advantage. This causal mechanism underwrites inequality in income, growth of corruption, concentration of power, a hardening of social class divides and a long list of other social problems.

The structural problem lies with the observation that all social agents, from individuals to families to businesses and nations, predominantly try to leverage their competitive advantage. And if they refrain from doing so, they will gradually succumb to the evolutionary selection mechanisms of 'survival of the fittest.' This means that the greatest competitive advantage is acquired through a self-reinforcing feedback mechanism that amplifies an already acquired advantage, to an even more advantageous one. More wants more and more gets more...

The narrative that platforms and the Internet at large have a democratizing effect routinely resurfaces, as users on social platforms all have access to a public bullhorn—or so the saying goes. Attracted attention is far from equally distributed among online users. Following the insight of Herbert Simon, it isn't of interest whether everyone or the majority has an online voice: *What is essential here, is whether ones' voice is*

Fig. 2.2 Unpaid bills, a race to the bottom—meme on the unintended consequences of the Matthew effect—inspired by the movie Grease (1978) with the hit duet, "You're the one that I want" with Olivia Newton John and John Travolta

being heard—and that is an entirely different matter (Fig. 2.2).

With the Matthew effect in mind, it is no surprise that online attention doesn't follow a normal distribution like the graphs of say height, weight and intelligence, where the majority of users are located in a wide center except for the few outliers at the ends, who either receive an outsized amount of attention or none at all. Online attention follows a power law distribution (Webster 2014). Only a few stock a lot of attention, and typically accumulate even more, while all others are dotted up and down the tail end of this power law distribution. To be sure, a majority of online traffic is in the hands and firmly controlled by a handful or two large corporations, depending on how these conglomerates are tallied up and categorized: Meta/Facebook, Google, YouTube, Amazon, Apple, Microsoft, etc. have and control most of the traffic.[2] And those who are already big are getting even bigger: Facebook acquired Instagram and WhatsApp and is now

[2] Patel, D. (2020). "Tech companies are 'too big, and we've allowed them to exercise monopoly power,'" says House Antitrust chairman David Cicilline, *The Verge*, 23.01.2020, verified 06.07.2020:

https://www.theverge.com/2020/1/23/21078903/podcast-house-antitrust-chairman-cicillinetech-monopoly-vergecast all Meta, Google bought YouTube and a few years ago Jeff Bezos, founder and majority shareholder of Amazon, added an unusual acquisition to his portfolio—*The Washington Post*. Although Amazon is best known for selling everything from bags, books and beauty products, Bezos bought one of the most renowned newspapers in the world—complete with journalists, inkwells, goose feathers and all.

In this sense, both news and politics potentially become the products being sold. This wasn't wasted on the late president Donald J. Trump when he aimed his anger, once again, at *The Washington Post*, about something the paper had written about him in 2018. Rather than attacking the newspaper directly, Trump used Twitter to accuse Amazon of unfair competition with the United States Postal Service, as both deliver parcels across the US. On the following trading day Amazon stock dropped \$60 billion.[3] Leveraging financial damage on Amazon was a seemingly indirect but incredibly efficient way of settling a political feud with *The Washington Post*.

In any event, the tale provides a glimpse of the complexity of the information ecosystem that everyone from social platforms to the established press are entrenched. And there is more where that came from. Several social platforms and tech businesses have novel information-borne products in the pipeline: everything from news and movies to games and currencies. More products are being launched and market shares are growing, but they're falling into ever fewer and fewer hands.

In this sense the structural mechanism of the attention economy's Matthew principle can be regrettably slanted.

---

[3] Wagner, J. (2018). "Trump levels false attacks against The Post and Amazon in a pair of tweets", *The Washington Post*, 23.07.2018, verified 06.07.2020: https://www.washingtonpost.com/politics/trump-levels-false-attacks-against-the-post-and-amazon-in-a-pair-of-tweets/2018/07/23/16d2fc68-8e84-11e8-b769-e3fff17f0689_story.html

Assume now that all social interaction may be cynically boiled down to maximizing competitive advantages, either directly by exerting power or indirectly by strengthening the feedback loop. If someone, for instance, acquired firm control over the executive branch, it's a short leap to conquering legislative power and even shorter to accruing total control. If, on the other hand, it becomes evident that there are delayed unfavorable consequences and side effects, such as increased corruption, then these too will grow in the loop as the system self-corrects, until it all collapses.

The sustainability problem is a side effect of the human ambition to maximize ones' competitive advantage. Whether this behavior relates to environment, economy or social relations, the crux of sustainability lies with the capacity to retain a particular behavior infinitely. Moreover, when it comes to politics, economics, climate change, social inequality, social relations, culture or even the slicing of a cake, the sustainability problem may become an adverse byproduct of the constant attempt to maximize ones competitive advantage, as the self-reinforcing effects can initiate a race to the bottom rather than to the top.

Tristan Harris, the American cofounder of Center for Humane Technology in Washington D.C. and prior design ethicist at Google, calls the business model of the attention economy a race to the bottom of the brain stem:

> It's not because anyone is evil or has bad intentions. It's because the game is getting attention at all costs. And the problem is it becomes this race to the bottom of the brainstem, where if I go lower on the brainstem to get you, you know, using my product, I win.[4]

---

[4] Cooper, A. (2017). "What is brain haching? Tech insiders on why you should care", *60 Minutes*, 09.04.2017, verified 16.05.2021: https://www.cbsnews.com/news/brain-hacking-tech-insiders-60-minutes/

The battle for attention is on unequal footing. On one side of the screen are the users. On the other side of the screen are the more or less concealed behavioral designs of the tech platforms, developed by thousands of programmers and psychologists, to capture and retain the attention of their users. "Technology dictates what billions of people see every day. Technology plays chess with your brain, and you lose," says Harris (Mehlsen 2020). Harris is one of the main sources in Jeff Orlowskis popular Netflix-documentary *The Social Dilemma* from 2020, where apostates from Google, YouTube, Facebook, Twitter and Instagram go on the record to tell how platform designs can influence human behavior as well as democracy itself.

In April 2021, Tristan Harris testified before the US congress during the senate hearing 'Algorithms and Amplification,' to explain how algorithms spread online content and thereby amplify opinions in public debate. Here Harris made clear that the negative influence of social media platforms on users is not merely about whether the platforms permit or remove misinformation, harmful content or controversial profiles. The negative influence is baked into the business model of the attention economy itself:

> As *The Social Dilemma* explains, the problem is their attention-harvesting business model. The narrower and more personalized our feeds, the fatter their bank accounts, and the more degraded the capacity of the American brain. The more money they make, the less capacity America has to define itself as America, reversing the United States inspiring and unifying motto of *E Pluribus Unum* or "out of many, one" into its opposite, "out of one, many."[5]

---

[5] Sub-committee on Privacy, Technology, and the Law (2021). "Algorithms and Amplification: How Social Media Platforms' Design Choices Shape Our Discourse and Our Minds", 27.04.2021, verified 13.06.2021: https://www.judiciary.senate.gov/meetings/algorithms-and-amplification-how-social-media-platforms-design-choices-shape-our-discourse-and-our-minds

In an attention economy it may very well turn into a race to the bottom for social platforms and their users. If competitive advantage becomes a question of how to maximize the amount of attention that can be paid or received, then the primary goal will be to bet on information that users are willing to spend their frugal attention on. Consequently, information providers may be tempted to ignore poor quality information, as long as it's consumed precisely as former Facebook employee Frances Haugen argued in the WSJ's *Facebook Files* in October 2021.

2.5   Good and Bad Information Products

The current state of the information market attention economy is comparable to the situation of the financial markets in the 2000s (Hendricks 2017). Alan Greenspan, the Chair of the American Federal Reserve between 1987 and 2006, eagerly promoted what Hungarian-American businessman George Soros dubbed *market fundamentalism* i.e., the idea that a free and generally speaking unregulated market provides the conditions for growth, wealth, financial innovation and therefore plays a crucial role in solving societal and financial problems. Three related thesis largely fit this world view:

1. Free market agents are self-interested and utility maximizing.
2. Growth can be measured in GDP.
3. The purpose of government is to stimulate (1) and (2).

To this should be added the idea that every *laissez faire* market with self-interested and utility maximizing institutions and actors was *efficient* in the sense that incorrect pricing of products or services would self-correct given the liquidity of the market. The self-regulating effect would eventually put the market in a supply and demand equilibrium state in which only the financially sound and healthy products, companies and services would survive. Hence the free markets would in and by themselves provide the close to ideal conditions for growth and wealth without bubble formation and other financial abominations (Vogel 2010).

In the wake of the financial crisis 2007–2008, Alan Greenspan rather shockingly had to admit that deregulation and market fundamentalism couldn't quite cash in the expectations:

> I made a mistake in presuming that the self-interests of organizations, specifically banks and others, were such that they were best capable of protecting their own shareholders and their equity in the firms.[6]

Some of the godawful "equity" around at that time, which in the end did not protect the financial sector, shareholders and banks but rather turned out to be a key player in the financial meltdown was the *subprime business*. Subprime loans, that is poor quality loans without much or any security, were bought, repackaged, syndicated and subsequently handled by big financial players who in turn were allowed to sell and place bets on these imaginative high risk financial products. When they later stopped to look at the equity and take stock of what they actually had on the shelves, it became clear that things didn't look too good. What they at first thought was a golden nest egg, was merely poorly secured debt that would be incredibly difficult to collect. The debt then was seemingly not worth much and so, along with the markets, the

---

[6] Beattle, A. & Politi, J. (2008)."'I made a mistake', admits Greenspan"", *Financial Times*, 23.10.2008, verified 06.07.2020: https://www.ft.com/content/aee9e3a2-a11f-11dd-82fd-000077b07658

illusion burst. Nevertheless, in the liberal and deregulated market of the 2000s, these financial products gained considerable traction … at least for a while. No more rehearsal here of the subprime crisis due to lack of time but suffice it to say that *the subprime business should not be up for even dress rehearsal ever again.*

Similarly, there is a parallel idea of market fundamentalism governing the information marketplace:

1. Agents in the free information market are self-interested and utility maximizing.
2. Growth may be measured in (allocation of attention and) data-harvest.
3. The purpose of tech platforms is to stimulate (1) and (2).

A wide range of different agents, large and small, bring a multitude of information products of variable quality to the information market. Market bids on these information products are paid for with attention, which in turn provides engagement, traffic, and data… the rest of the business model is familiar by now. But just because the market is liquid and trades an incredible amount of information for attention, does not necessarily entail, as seen in case of the *laissez faire*-market of finance, that the information market is efficient in the sense that only healthy and strong information products survive while the weak and faulty perish in the tough competition for attention. There exists a market for poor quality information products—at times of extremely poor quality—that nonetheless are capable of attracting scores and scores of attention regardless of whether the information is true or false. Whatever is true is not necessarily viral, and whatever is viral is not necessarily true (Hendricks 2016). An implication of (2) is exactly that increased media usage is identified with progress no matter the content consumed.

Just to be clear—the structure and dynamics of the information market ruled by an attention economy immediately lends itself to a market for fake news, misinformation and bullshit. At least four reasons may be given for entering this market (Hendricks and Vestergaard 2019):

- for the fun of it/trolling;
- propaganda/power struggles;
- marketing/advertising;
- web traffic/money.

The issuing parties of fake news want to allocate people's attention—they may even be working on commission for the advertisers. The greater the allocation of attention, guaranteed by noisy and spectacular but not necessarily true news story, the more you may jack up the prices for advertising online for whatever the reason; for fun, political influence, advertising or just immediate cash money. Fake news is a poor information product as subprime loans were poor financial products. But just like sub-primes could survive for quite some time on deregulated financial markets … so can fake news live and prosper in terms of attention on a non-regulated information market. There is no ordinance in the course of being appraised to the effect that the information exchanged online has to be true. The information market doesn't necessarily find a natural equilibrium in which only the correct information will strive and the fake will get weeded out due to the liquidity of the market. And there we have it: *Happy Hour for fake news.*

Akin to poor financial products such as subprime loans, toxic information products may likewise be seen as poorly secured assets based on unreliable information sources. Say information that willingly and with intent, or unknowingly and without intent, combines truth with falsehoods and bullshit; information that stimulates undocumented subversive rumors, consolidates conspiracies; information that forges weaponized narratives, distorts, silences, stokes division and creates polarization while aggravating crowds to the point of action and insurrection. All spectacularly packaged into soundbites, images and deepfake videos that attract enormous loads and loads of attention, regardless of whether the information products in the end can pass an evidential check and stand up to source transparency while getting the facts straight. As long as it trends, it's true ...

3

Designed Denial: Infodemics and Fake News

"If you can make it trend, you can make it true."

– Renee DiResta

Fake news is not a new phenomenon, but the fast and far-reaching spread of it is a new feature of the digital world. In the information age fake news is like a magnet in the attention economy and quite toxic for the information market as such.

Social platforms have seen an explosion of fake news and misinformation in connection with the global outbreak of coronavirus. In parallel with the Covid-19 pandemic, a veritable 'infodemic' unfolded and is still ongoing.[1] Misinformation is sort of like a virus; it spreads in similar patterns but even faster and with higher contact numbers and infection rates than a disease pandemic.

Fabulously fantasy filled stories may spread so rapidly and so deep that they influence people's behavior and state of health. They add fuel to fires of vaccine skepticism, spark

---

[1] WHO (2020). "Infodemic", verified 06.01.2022: https://www.who.int/health-topics/infodemic#tab=tab_1

© The Author(s), under exclusive license to Springer Nature Switzerland AG 2022
V. F. Hendricks, C. Mehlsen, *The Ministry of Truth*,
https://doi.org/10.1007/978-3-030-98629-2_3

mistrust towards health authorities as well as political leaderships and foment public protests and riots. With the arrival of the infodemic, social platforms have become more intensively involved in the fight against spreading misinformation, fake news and bullshit, and they try, to an ever greater extent, to control which narratives get into circulation.

3.1   Infodemic

> **BREAKING – BREAKING – BREAKING – BREAKING**
> *Coronavirus is a biological weapon developed by the Americans against the Chinese — a weapon that only affects the Mongolian race and the Hollywood-film* Contagion, *with Laurence Fishburne, Gwyneth Paltrow and Jude Law, is partly evidence to the effect that coronavirus is an American invention.*

In the wake of the first outbreak of coronavirus, many unfounded rumors and stories flourished about why the world was experiencing a pandemic. It may come as a surprise how a conspiracy theory, about the film *Contagion* and Covid-19 as a biological weapon against the Mongolian race, could emerge and become widespread on social media platforms, especially when the movie is from 2011.

What started as a medical crisis, shortly thereafter became an information crisis. As the general director of WHO, Tedros Adhanom Ghereyesus, said in February 2020:

> We aren't just battling the virus; we are also battling the trolls and conspiracy theorists that push misinformation and undermine the outbreak response.[2]

---

[2] WHO (2020). "Director-General's remarks at the media briefing on 2019 novel coronavirus on 8 February 2020", verified 16.05.2021: https://www.who.int/director-general/speeches/detail/director-general-s-remarks-at-the-media-briefing-on-2019-novel-coronavirus%2D%2D-8-february-2020

What happens online has consequences offline. In the United States a person died after drinking an aquarium cleaning product that contained chloroquine. Chloroquine, which is often used to fight malaria, was claimed by some users on social platforms to fight off Covid-19, among the proponents of this belief was Brazilian president Jair Bolsonaro. In Iran, hundreds of people died from drinking methanol after it was hailed as a panacea against Covid-19 on social platforms.[3]

Theories are also circulating that Americans (or the Chinese—depending on what side voted for) are responsible for Covid-19 as part of their biological warfare program; that coronavirus was put into the world as part of a conspiracy between the English Pirbright Institute and Bill Gates to control global population growth… and so on.

In 2020 the Ukraine Crisis Media Center published a catalog of the most widespread misinformation stories and conspiracy theories that circulated during the first months of the Covid-19 pandemic.[4] Along with coronavirus as a biological weapon one can find, among others, these extravagant explanations on social media:

- Coronavirus is just a normal flu.
- Coronavirus is the EU's revenge for Brexit.
- Coronavirus is designed to promote mandatory vaccination programs.
- Coronavirus is a Zionistic plot.

---

[3] Shokoohi, M., Nasiri, N., Sharifi, H., Barai, S. & Stranges, S. (2020). "A syndemic of COVID-19 and methanol poisoning in Iran: Time for Iran to consider alcohol use as a public health challenge?", *Alcohol*, 2020 Sep; 87: 25–27, verified: https://www.ncbi.nlm.nih.gov/pmc/articles/PMC7272173/

[4] "Top conspiracy theories on coronavirus", Hybrid Warfare Analytical Group, Ukraine Crisis Media Center, 22.04.2020: https://uacrisis.org/en/top-conspiracy-theories-on-coronavirus. Similar listings are to be found with Los Alamos National Laboratory: "New AI tool tracks evolution of COVID-19 conspiracy theories on social media", 19.04.2021: https://www.eurekalert.org/pub_releases/2021-04/danl-na041921.php

- Coronavirus is orchestrated by the pharmaceutical industry to generate profit.
- Coronavirus is an economic conspiracy against the aging population.
- Coronavirus is caused by 5G-network.
- Coronavirus is created by the Democratic party in the USA to get rid of Trump.
- Coronavirus is financed by Microsoft founder Bill Gates so he can sell his own vaccine.
- Coronavirus is a ploy for liberal democratic governments to install a police state.
- Coronavirus was developed to stop the climate crisis.

Many different agents and motives are responsible for launching these types of stories and for acting as "superspreaders" and "superspreader events".[5]

Ironically and tragically, even though the Ukraine Crisis Media Center is responsible for collecting the information mentioned above on Covid-19 conspiracy theories, a recent report from the United Nations Development Program (UNDP) and the United Nations Children's Fund (UNICEF), found that Ukrainian lives are likely in danger as a result of the infodemic of false and misleading information. In the period from March to November 2020, researchers studied around 30 million messages from Ukrainians on social platforms with the help of SemanticForce, an advanced monitoring and analysis tool. The study identified approximately 250,000 messages with Covid-19 related misinformation on online media, blogs, discussion forums and social networks within Ukraine. Furthermore, the study found that

---

[5] Klepper, D., Amiri, F. & Dupuy, B. (2021). "The superspreaders behind top COVID-19 conspiracy theories", *Associated Press* (in cooperation with Atlantic Council's Digital Forensic Research Lab), 15.01.2021, verified 25.04.2021: https://apnews.com/article/conspiracy-theories-iran-only-on-ap-media-misinformation-bfca6d5b236a29d61c4dd38702495ffe

these false stories minimized citizens' willingness to follow the recommendations of authorities to keep a proper distance, to wear a mask, to sanitize hands and so on. At the same time they were less likely to recommend vaccination to vulnerable people in their social circle. The researchers behind the study therefore concluded that an uncontrollable infodemic could significantly increase the population's exposure to Covid-19.[6]

The problem however is far from unique to Ukraine. A global study from 2020 examined 100 million Facebook users' views on vaccines. It showed that 6.9 million users were for vaccines and 4.2 million users were against them, but also that the anti-vaccine group, often under the influence of misinformation, had the most interactions with the rest of the 74.1 million who didn't take a stand. These so-called "swing-vaxxers" have been, and will continue to be, very important for health organizations to reach out to—not just in connection with Covid-19, but also when and if future pandemics hit.[7]

Mistrust and uncertainty with respect to health authorities' recommendations and views on vaccines related to Covid-19 is largely prompted by the information available. But how do you sort dirt from ground cinnamon or lies from truth?

---

[6] "'Infodemic' of COVID-19 disinformation bad for Ukrainians health, study for UN finds [EN/UK]", OCHA: Reliefweb, 03.03.2021, verified 26.04.2021: https://reliefweb.int/report/ukraine/infodemic-covid-19-disinformation-bad-ukrainians-health-study-un-finds-enuk

[7] WHO (2020). "Immunizing the public against misinformation", 25.08.2020, verified 26.04.2021: https://www.who.int/news-room/feature-stories/detail/immunizing-the-public-against-misinformation

3.2   The Quality
of Information Products

Fake news is an example of an information product that may indeed have dire consequences. It is not just for fun that the World Economic Forum, since 2013, has emphasized the threat of fake news in its annual risk report; the FN, EU, OECD have also voiced similar warnings:

> The global risk of *massive digital misinformation* sits at the center of a constellation of technological and geopolitical risks ranging from *terrorism* to *cyber attacks* and *the failure of global governance*.[8]

Fake news has existed as long as there has been a press—most likely also before, when wild rumors and good stories swirled around the camp fire. The *new* thing is that fake news occupies more and more of the media landscape and spreads quickly to a large and global audience via social media platforms and mobile apps. The method and speed with which fake news may spread in the global digital information structure, is a new condition of historical proportions. An insightful and very thorough study of Twitter data, published in *Science* in 2018, shows that false information spreads further and faster than truthful information. At the same time, and contrary to popular belief, the study shows that rather than bots and algorithms, it is us humans who are prone to spreading misinformation (Vosoughi et al. 2018).

A defining feature of fake news is that its purpose is something other than sound journalism and informing the public. Fake news *pretend* to be abide to journalistic principles and

---

[8] World Economic Forum (2013). "Digital Wildfires in a Hyperconnected World", verified 16.05.2021: https://reports.weforum.org/global-risks-2013/risk-case-1/digital-wildfires-in-a-hyperconnected-world/

truth-tracking but in reality is something totally different. In reality it is about misleading, setting the agenda of the day, propagandizing or bringing in money. Fake news, for example, can originate from seemingly well-established URLs ("abcnews.com.co" instead of the correct address, abcnews. com), which are supplemented with witness accounts featuring manipulated images or video footage.

Fake news may be arranged on an information quality scale (Table 3.1). In Zone 1 are true statements that correspond to verified facts. If you say, "36% in U.S. have a "great deal" or "fair amount" of trust in mass media" then this statement is true if a reliable method—such as the one used by *Gallup 2021 Survey*—confirms these numbers.[9]

Table 3.1 Information quality scale from true statements to rumors, bullshit and fake news (Hendricks and Vestergaard 2019)

ZONE 1	
True statements	Verified facts
ZONE 2	
Doctored statements	Framing, exaggeration, omission, cherry-picking of facts
Undocumented statements	Rumors (maybe true, maybe false)
ZONE 3	
False statements	Misrepresentation of, and contrary to, the facts
Lies	Intended false statements
Bullshit	Misrepresentation of motives and purpose, pretense, feigning, dissolution of the dividing line between true and false
Fake news	Feigned news, misrepresentation of motives and purpose simulating journalism and truthfulness

---

[9] Brenan, M. (2021). "Americans' Trust in Media Dips to Second Lowest on Record", *Gallup – Politics*, 07.10.2021, verified 06.01.2022: https://news.gallup.com/poll/355526/americans-trust-media-dips-second-lowest-record.aspx

Zone 2 includes doctored statements that are neither directly false nor completely true—it depends on how you look at it. Is it, for example, more true to say 90% of the workforce enjoys employment than to state a 10% unemployment rate? It adds up to 100% either way, but may sound very differently, depending on one's view on the labor market conditions and labor market policy. This type of so-called *framing* has shown to be decisive for how people choose a stance, even though the net result is the same (Kahneman & Tversky 1979).

In Zone 2, in addition to framing, exaggerations and omissions, there is the use of selective truth, where you refer to parts of the truth which benefits your agenda and omit the rest—the truth is cherry-picked. Nick Clegg, former Deputy Prime Minister of Great Britain and, since 2018, responsible for global affairs and communication at Meta/Facebook, stated recently that *virality* is the cause of fake news and misinformation on the Internet.[7] At the same time, he seems comfortable omitting that it is mostly Facebook itself that has the ability to control virality. Clegg thus misinforms without actually saying anything false. In addition, Zone 2 also includes undocumented statements, which may be true, may be false, such as rumors, where there simply isn't enough information available to definitely determine the truth value of the statements in question.

Zone 3 contains the deliberately misleading statements starting with a lie which is the least toxic of the bunch. It is often rehearsed that misinformation is false and that fake news is indeed fake. However, this presupposes that there's a clean distinction between true and false generally accepted and agreed upon and possible to uphold. Even a liar is in a sense sincere since if the distinction between true and false is not maintained, it is impossible to define what a lie is. So it might well be that a liar says the polar opposite of the truth, in order to cheat, discredit, deceive or give others a false impression, well knowing that it isn't the truth—but it doesn't change the fact that one thing is false while the other is true.

Even ancient Academic skepticism accept the distinction. Carneades and Arcesilaus whom, in 200 BC. led the Platonic Academy in ancient Greece, followed the Socratic dictum that the only thing they know is that they don't know. Despite, or rather because of, this predicament, they indeed accepted the distinction between true and false. Otherwise they had no way of knowing that they knew nothing, as this statement presumably is *true*. Documented throughout the history of philosophy, the same logic applies to all the arguments that skeptics have leveraged against knowledge. They basically all rely on presenting relevant possibilities of error to the effect that our perception of the world is plain wrong and misguided, but that this very possibility of error also suggests that something is correct, i.e. true (Hendricks 2006). Different relativistic derivatives of skepticism that see truth as a function of a particular paradigm, culture, class, true-for-one-false-for-another, still subscribe to upholding the distinction between true and false.

In 1986 Harry Frankfurt, an American philosopher at Princeton University, wrote the essay "On Bullshit", which was published as a book in a slightly reworked and expanded form in 2005. It has since become a bestseller translated into multiple languages around the world. *On Bullshit* is one of the foremost examples of linguistic philosophical analysis and precise rhetorical determination of a colloquial concept. Frankfurt forcefully foments the real, tangible and severe epistemological consequences bullshit has for all of us cognitively and communicatively.

Bullshit is venomous to our way of seeing, understanding and acting in the world, individually and collectively. A bullshitter doesn't care about the distinction between true and false. True and false statements may be mixed at will, there is no obligation to maintain a distinction between them. Frankfurt's bullshitter bluffs, cheats, makes a lot of noise, and lies at will and without any connection to reality. That is the essence of bullshit:

> It is just this lack of connection to a concern with truth — this indifference to how things really are — that I regard as of the essence of bullshit. [...] For the essence of bullshit is not that it is false but that it is phony (Frankfurt 1986): 18

Fake news is thus either lies or bullshit, but it simulates journalism and thus truthfulness. Frankfurt recognized that there was a lot of bullshit already back in 1986 when the original essay was published, and in the digital information age there is hardly less bullshit floating around. The phenomenon is widespread today because there aren't always requirements for checks and balances on what you say, write and probably believe—and the more who apparently believe the same, the better, all of which is strengthened by the architecture and algorithmic information curation of social platforms. Stories that make noise and gain a lot of support is the success criterion in the attention economy. Whether it is true or false, is of little interest, if at all. At the same time it may be difficult to decide if a fake news story is true or false for real. And remember; don't believe anything you think.

Next level bullshit are the so-called deepfakes, where computer simulations combined with artificial intelligence instruments are used to falsify videos of people in such an effective way that it is virtually impossible to distinguish manipulated footage from the real deal. In 2018 and with help from easily accessible programs like Adobe After Effects and FakeApp, American actor, comedian and movie

Fig. 3.1 "A total and complete dipshit" is what a simulated and manipulated "Barack Obama" calls Donald J. Trump, but in fact it's comedian Jordan Peele and *Buzzfeed* behind this deepfake video

producer Jordan Peele together with *Buzzfeed* magazine was able to manipulate a video so that it appeared as though former President Barack Obama called Donald Trump "a total and complete dipshit" (Fig. 3.1).

The YouTube video is entitled "You won't believe what Obama says in this video!"—which indeed is unbelievably believable. The video was by many considered to herald the beginning of a new and dangerous era of "next-level bullshit", with deepfakes that may sow pervasive distrust in the press and material featuring on social platforms and the Internet at large. Deepfakes may also contribute to uncertainty, indecisiveness and cynicism, further intensifying the challenges of maintaining a sustainable public online-culture in democratic societies (Vaccari and Chadwick 2020).

3.3   Bias and Bots

With the arrival of the infodemic, tech platforms are fighting the spread of coronavirus misinformation more intensively. Twitter, Facebook and Google are working together with WHO and other health authorities to remove coronavirus misinformation. The platforms may opt to close or suspend profiles spreading malignant information.

Between January 2020—February 2021, Facebook removed more than 12 million bits of "misinformation, that may result in physical injury".[10] The following claims and narratives are examples of content that Facebook and Instagram categorize as misinformation and thus remove:

- Coronavirus is made or produced by humans.
- Covid-19 vaccines do not prevent the spread of the disease they are developed to protect against.
- It is safer to get the illness than the vaccine.
- Covid-19 vaccines are poisonous or dangerous and can lead to autism.

In the fight against misinformation the platforms not only remove content and shut down profiles, they also tweak a long list of parameters to limit the spread and visibility of misinformation (shadow banning) while amplifying the circulation of correct information from, among others, public health authorities and recognized researchers. In 2021 Facebook gave a $120 million advertising discount to health authorities, NGOs and UN organizations, so science-based information about coronavirus could reach more users. Just as Facebook informs its users about where they can vote in

---

[10] Jin, K.-X. (2021). "Reaching Billions of People With COVID-19 Vaccine Information", Facebook, 08.02.2021, verified 20.5.2021: https://about.fb.com/news/2021/02/reaching-billions-of-people-with-covid-19-vaccine-information/

national elections, the platform now also provides information about the nearest location for receiving vaccines.

Facebook has been using behavior modifying measures to prevent the spread of coronavirus, for example, by placing reminders to use a facemask, at the top of the screen when a user is on Facebook or Instagram. According to Facebook, they reached 26 million users through their #WearAMask campaign, which led to an increase in people who believed it to be important or very important to wear a mask in public.[11]

With Facebook and other social platforms awash with misinformation, and despite Facebook's efforts to fight coronavirus misinformation, the American President Joe Biden went on to accuse Facebook of "killing people" in July 2021. Biden's allegation applied, not the least, to the unvaccinated population who are skeptical of the Covid-19 vaccination program and the outbreak and takeover of the highly contagious delta variant of coronavirus at the time. Biden later softened his death sentence statement: Covid vaccine misinformation on Facebook "harms people" without directly killing them.[12] Facebook responded by rejecting the accusation and in their rebuttal they in fact "save lives"; they pointed to their Covid-19 information campaign and the more than two billion people reached via Facebook who were presented with reliable information related to Covid-19 and vaccines.[13] Regardless of whether Facebook "saves" more than it "harms,"

[11] Jin, K.-X. (2021). "Reaching Billions of People With COVID-19 Vaccine Information", Facebook, 08.02.2021, verified 20.5.2021: https://about.fb.com/news/2021/02/reaching-billions-of-people-with-covid-19-vaccine-information/

[12] Kelly, M. (2021). "Joe Biden says Facebook isn't 'killing people,' but misinformation causes harm", The Verge, 19.07.2021: https://www.theverge.com/2021/7/19/22583809/joe-biden-facebook-covid19-coronavirus-vaccine-misinformation-killing-people

[13] Bose, N. & Culliford, E. (2021). "Biden says Facebook, others 'killing people' by carrying COVID misinformation", Reuters, 17.07.2021, verified 18.07.2021: https://www.reuters.com/business/healthcare-pharmaceuticals/white-house-says-facebooks-steps-stop-vaccine-misinformation-are-inadequate-2021-07-16/

it sets a clear example that Facebook's measures affect human behavior to such an extent that it may indeed mean the difference between life and death.

Twitter has also modified different settings to dial down misinformation. In October 2020, before the American presidential election, Twitter experimented with the so-called "quote tweets" instead of the classic retweets. Instead of just sending a tweet further into circulation by retweeting it, users had to write a comment before sharing it.[14] Twitter hoped that the change would effectuate thoughtfulness and reflection before users boosted the tweet by sharing it.[15] It is a design feature from the strategic toolbox to stop the spread of misinformation by creating a so-called *friction* that makes it more difficult to react without thought.

It had a limited effect however. For even though the number of quote tweets rose, nearly 45% were just single word confirmations and 70% of the comments were less than 25 characters long. Thus, the comments didn't consist of especially detailed explanations on why something was passed on.[16] Nevertheless, it is an example of how social platforms attempt to change users' engagement incentives and behavior via subtle design changes within the user interface itself.

Interventions such as friction may be used to work *for us*, but they can equally be used to work against us, when one understands our cognitive dispositions and thus may speculate in how to leverage them. We are evolutionarily predisposed to a number of cognitive biases which, among other

---

[14] Twitter Support (2020). Tweet, 09.10.2020, verified 25.06.2021: https://twitter.com/twittersupport/status/1339350336184541184?lang=en

[15] Twitter (2020). "How to Retweet", Twitter, verified 19.05.2021: https://help.twitter.com/en/using-twitter/how-to-retweet

[16] APB News Bureau (2020). "Good Old Retweet Button Is Back On Twitter! Netizens Welcome The Decision With Funniest Memes", *APB News*, 17.12.2020, verified 17.05.2021: https://news.abplive.com/news/gadgets/good-old-retweet-button-is-back-on-twitter-netizens-welcome-the-decision-with-funniest-memes-1413909

things, mean that we prefer information from people we already know in our so-called *in-group* (Aronson et al. 2015). Furthermore, we are very aware of and share information about what we perceive as a risk to our safety while we often enough search for, and remember information, that is consistent with what we already understand and believe.

On tech platforms, the implemented information technologies may amplify these cognitive biases in inappropriate ways, such as:

- Social platforms, search engines and news portals operate on the basis of personalized user-based recommendation algorithms that preferentially provide information from a very narrow subset of sources which are often algorithmically promoted by popularity rather than quality (Ciampaglia et al. 2018).
- Social platforms often connect like-minded people and those who agree with one another, which gives rise to polarization, echo chamber effects (Conover et al. 2012) and isolated opinion environments without appreciable information-based interaction (Sasahara et al. 2021).
- Social platforms may promote reactionary opinions. Information that is shared in the social network not only increases bias, it becomes more resistant to potential adjustments or outright corrections when more balanced information is presented (Jagiello and Hills 2018).

Making things worse is that bots, automated profiles on social platforms, and which appear to be controlled by real people, may increase already unfortunate tendencies of behavior and take advantage of our cognitive vulnerabilities. And it doesn't take much: In a computer simulation conducted by researchers, at the University of Warwick in England and the Observatory on Social Media at Indiana

University, Bloomington, in the U.S., bots were included in a social network as agents which could only tweet memes of poor information quality and could only retweet each other. The result was that when less than 1% of people followed these bots, the information quality in the network remained high. However as soon as bot infiltration exceeded 1%, poor information quality spread in the network (Yan et al. 2020). In real social networks it turns out that just a couple of well-placed early reactions from bots can result in a fake news story going viral (Glenski and Weninger 2017). Bots can thereby quickly pollute the otherwise desirable free market-place of thoughts and ideas. They can massively amplify the social influence of machines on people (Hagen et al. 2020). In 2017 it was estimated that up to 15% of all active Twitter accounts were bots and that these accounts played crucial roles in the spread of misinformation during the American presidential election in 2016 (Shao et al. 2018).

Computer simulations further documented that the ability to detect bots is also a function of one's bias—for example, political bias, which manifests itself in a rather amusing and asymmetric way: Republicans are more likely to confuse bots that promote conservative ideas for people, while Democrats have a tendency to confuse conservatives with bots (Yan et al. 2020).

There exists an ingenious network of false Twitter profiles that plays on both sides of the aisle: Fake news sites and bots are used to drive political polarization forward and at the same time drive the lucrative business of advertisement sales. All of it is steered by a single entity, where some bots and sites act as Trump MAGA (Make America Great Again) supporters, while others bear a striking resemblance to Trump opponents. Both parties ask for campaign donations to their respective endeavors, even though their endeavors are really one and the same—polarization and profit (Pacheo, D. Hui,

P.-M, Torres-Lugo et al. 2021). Humans can do it too—buying your way to promote content by using clickbait farms where clickbait actors make money on promoting particular agendas via ad revenues sometimes funded directly by various BigTech companies through entangled and untransparent ad-tech architectures.[17]

3.4   Information that Works and Distorts

As part of our evolutionarily developed cognitive bias we often make use of quick estimates and immediate assessments, as cognitive shortcuts i.e., *heuristics*, in our pursuit to determine what is true and what is false. Much of the information in our everyday life and immediate environment is immediately true: There is a cyclist I have to avoid because I can see that he hasn't seen me; I can see that the dairy section in the grocery store is down the aisle to the right. If these immediate observations weren't true, it would be exceedingly difficult to navigate through the city streets and to secure whole milk for your cornflakes.

We also have other shortcuts that encourage information to find its way into human consciousness. These heuristics are often very effective and quite reliable in search for the correct answer (Kahneman 2011). They may, however, also lead us astray and towards misinformation, bullshit and fake news. The ways that social platforms sort and promote information, with an eye for our continued engagement, doesn't make it easier for us to navigate cognitive shortcuts.

---

[17] Hao, K. (2021). "How Facebook and Google fund Global Misinformation", *MIT Technology Review*, 20.11.2021, verified 17.01.2022: https://www.technologyreview.com/2021/11/20/1039076/facebook-google-disinformation-clickbait/

Low quality information tends to easily find its way to our consciousness, as our cognitive heuristics react to information in a certain order:

- **Information which is new**. Newsworthiness and hype have an advantage in the attention economy; they spread faster than old information and also go deeper in the way that they can alter our beliefs, change our behavior and strengthen our ability to predict (Aral 2020). A ten year-long study of users' habits on Twitter showed that reactions of surprise, as an indication that the information is new, are more frequently found in people who react to fake news stories than to truthful ones (Vosoughi et al. 2018). Tech platforms stimulate the attention economy by placing new and fresh information at the top of our newsfeeds and search results. New information, at the same time, becomes more enticing in uncertain times, which is also apparent during the coronavirus crisis. While researchers worked intensely to find a vaccine, attention grabbing suggestions for alternative methods, ranging from garlic cures and vitamin supplements to hydroxychloroquine intake as remedies against the pandemic, abounded.[18]
- **Information which supports existing beliefs**. Humans have a tendency to accept information that fits with what we already believe. The likely reason for this is that because we perceive it as safe, it doesn't require much verification and mental expenditure from us. However, we often confuse facts with opinions. Information that supports one's preconceived notions is, after all, "out there on the web"

---

[18] Samuels, E. & Kelly, M. (2020). "How false hope spread about hydroxychloroquine to treat covid-19—and the consequences that followed", *Washington Post*, 13.04.2020, verified 25.06.2021: https://www.washingtonpost.com/politics/2020/04/13/how-false-hope-spread-about-hydroxychloroquine-its-consequences/

and is only further supported by the algorithmic curation of social platforms (Brashier and Marsh 2020).

- **Repeated information**. Even the most insane idea or theory appears less insane the more it is repeated. It is a tendency called the *illusory truth effect,* which is robustly documented (Unkelbach et al. 2019). Repostings on Facebook or retweets on Twitter are information repetition *par excellence.* When former President Donald J. Trump tweeted a link to a video, where a doctor fraudulently claimed that hydroxychloroquine cures Covid-19, the number of similar tweets exploded to over a million the following day alone.[19]

- **Information arousing feelings**. Anger, anxiety and disgust capture the attention of users. An analysis of 126.000 cases of rumors found that false rumors have a greater likelihood of spreading disgust than truthful information (Vosoughi et al. 2018). False news can be shocking, surprising, anger inducing, and combined with eventual news worthiness, may spread faster and wider than truthful news.[20] Emotionally charged language alone may amplify the spread of messages on social platforms with up to 20% for every emotionally charged word used (Brady et al. 2017). Furthermore, when people defer to fluctuations on their emotional barometer to evaluate the truthfulness of a news story, they are more likely to be duped by fake news and misinformation (Martel et al. 2020).

---

[19] Mackey, T.M., Purushothaman, V., Haupt, M., Nali, M.C., Li, J. (2021). Comment: "Application of unsupervised machine learning to identify and characterise hydroxychloroquine misinformation on Twitter", *The Lancet*, 01.02.2021, verified 19.05.2021: https://www.thelancet.com/journals/landig/article/PIIS2589-7500(20)30318-6/fulltext

[20] Ritzau (2021). "Rettelser på Twitter fører til mere falsk information", *MediaWatch*, 30.05.2021, verified 01.06.2021: https://mediawatch.dk/Medienyt/politik/article13016627.ece?utm_campaign=MediaWatch%20Middag&utm_content=2021-05-31&utm_medium=email&utm_source=mediawatch

Given how our cognitive heuristics work, it is not surprising that some stories are given a disproportionate amount of attention, even if they are false.

Jonah Berger, American professor in marketing at The Wharton School, University of Pennsylvania, conducted a virality analysis of thousands of news articles and hundreds of brands. From this, he formulated a general model for the virality of online stories that may be broken down into six principles **S.T.E.P.P.S** (Berger 2013):

- **S**ocial Currency: The story should make people, who know or share the story, seem important in a way that conveys social status.
- **T**riggers: The story should get us to associate one phenomenon with another, just as the word "peanut butter" gets us to think of "jelly", or #metoo leads us to think about Harvey Weinstein's scandalous behavior, which propelled the movement in the U.S. and spread the world over, while #icantbreathe recalls thoughts of George Floyd's tragic death under police custody and which brought further momentum to #BlackLivesMatter.
- **E**motion: The story should spark emotions regardless of whether these are positive or negative.
- **P**ublic: The story needs to capture the interest of a broad public conversation and connect with commonly known interests and narratives.
- **P**ractical Value: The story should have an immediate practical value e.g., buying, eating, experiencing or meaning something, like offering good advice or recommendations.
- **S**tories: The story should be good, easy to follow, retell and have a simple dramaturgical composition.

Among these six principles *truth* is alarmingly absent. Although truth doesn't play a role in virality, emotions or sentiments do. Berger and his colleagues specifically found that news stories eliciting positive emotions, such as fascination and awe, are shared more often than negative stories with depressing or unhappy content (Berger and Milkman 2009). On a similar viral hierarchy level as fascination and awe-inspiring stories, lie a handful of other so-called *activity mobilizing emotions*, namely *anger, fear, indignation* and *resentment*, which mobilize the individual to act, share or comment. They have a degree of social transmission that largely resemble fascination and awe-inspiring stories.

If, in a fit of joy, you post, "I'm so happy today!" there probably won't be many who'll feel compelled to share or comment— well, family and close friends may respond with a "Good for you!"—what else is there to do? Joy or happiness are not activity mobilizing emotions; they are just states that you may find yourself in; they don't animate or mobilize others to do anything. On the other hand, if you write, for example "My CEO is an a**hole", "Donald Trump is a total and complete dipshit", #Stopthesteal, #thebiglie are different stories altogether. People tend to react by sharing, commenting or engaging in some other way when it comes to such stories. Content raising anger, as well as fear, resentment and indignation, are emotions that animate and motivate us to express our opinions, click, share and care and maybe even act, depending on what is at stake. Recently it came to light that Meta/Facebook have been tuning their point-systems for content in such a way that extra value was given to emoji-reactions like "angry" accordingly pushing emotional and provocative content into user news feeds in significant proportion—5 points for "angry", 1 point for a "like"—fostering rage as well as misinformation.[21]

---

[21] Merrill, J.B. & Oremus, W. (2021). "Five points for anger, one for a 'like': How Facebook's formula fostered rage and misinformation", *The Washington Post*, 26.10.2021: https://www.washingtonpost.com/technology/2021/10/26/facebook-angry-emoji-algorithm/Allenby, B. & Garreau (2017). "Weaponized Narrative is the New Battlespace", *Defense One*, 03.01.2017, verified 09.03.2022: https://www.defenseone.com/ideas/2017/01/weaponized-narrative-new-battlespace/134284/

Feeding into people's fear and anger is in no small measure also the business of "weaponized narratives" as they feature in information warfare. Beyond armaments, troop deployments, airstrikes and immediately devastating collateral damage, summary executions of civilians and non-combatants and war crimes in scale, weaponized narratives are intended to turn us against each other in times of conflict to undermine the opponent's culture, civilization, identity, will and hegemony. They are put in circulation on the information battlefield to stoke division, create confusion, mute, mesmerize or manipulate the media, misinform publics on both sides of the conflict sharpening the divide using potent us-versus-them manoeuvres inside as well as outside the information borne infrastructure. A potentially useful tool for autocratic rule with mass mis- and disinformation ambitions in order to reign and rule as so manifestly demonstrated during the Russian invasion of Ukraine in 2022 and the Kremlin command of Vladimir Putin.

3.5   From Information Stimuli to Behavioral Change

There is little doubt that information stimuli can elicit behavioral change, but precisely how, how much and in what way, remains scientifically underexplored. This is partly due to the many moving parts (motive, bias, social influence, context, etc.) that either completely or partially inform explanations of behavioral change, that cannot be reduced to information stimuli of (mis)information, bullshit or fake news.

Tyushka, A. (2021). " Weaponizing narrative: Russia contesting EUrope's liberal identity, *Journal of Contemporary European Studies*, 30:1, 115-135, https://doi.org/10.1080/14782804 2021.1883561

However, a study published in mid-2021 in the reputable journal *Computers in Human Behavior*, seemingly indicates that just 5 min of exposure to false information may subconsciously affect a person's behavior. At a French university, 233 students, between the ages of 17–21, participated in an experiment designed to test if reading a fake news story could subconsciously affect their behavior. As a measure of subconscious behavior itself, the students had to undergo a cognitive and motor test called the finger tapping test (FTT), where subjects had to repeatedly and as fast as possible press a keyboard key. Initially, all students were asked to complete a FTT in order to determine their maximum tapping speed or MTS. They were then randomly divided into three groups: a group that read a fabricated positive news story claiming that a high MTS is a trait associated with people who are successful; another group read a fabricated negative news story that claimed fast MTS is associated with deviant and brutal behavior. The third group, the control group, read a text with no mention of MTS.

Depending on which fabricated news story they were exposed to, the students used the keyboard differently. Students that read the positive news story showed an increase in MTS of a little over 5% (also when corrected for training effects), while the group that read the negative news story showed a decrease in their MTS by about 1.5%, which was not statistically significant relative to the control group. At the same time, the test subjects were quite unaware that the news stories could have influenced their behavior.

The average exposure time to the news stories was less than 5 min, which suggests, according to the study, that a fairly limited degree of exposure to false information can imperceptibly and underhandedly modify behavior.

Even though this was only an experiment, a large-scale information campaign could have just as effective an impact on voters. It could have changed the margin of the majority vote (the popular vote) in at least two American presidential campaigns: In 2016 the margin for the popular vote was 2.09%, while it was 3.86% in 2012 (Bastick 2021). This might seem negligible, but a few votes can sometimes decide the outcome of an election. Consider the presidential election of 2000, where Republican George W. Bush became president after a recount of the votes in the swing state of Florida. Bush won with a margin of 537 votes (equivalent to 0.009% of the approximately 6 million votes cast in Florida).

The manner in which social platforms handle the flow of information can be decisive to which stories come into circulation and enter public debate. By tweaking information and algorithms, platforms are able to design their way in and out of quite a lot which affect our interaction with information and determine our behavior in general.

At the same time platforms routinely claim that they don't want to decide what people can say or do online. Yet users are not necessarily able to write and behave as they wish and see fit without being locked out, hamstrung or censored, or opt out of facemask or vaccine site "advertisements". The ambiguity is not diminished by the platforms' ever changing positions on what content deserves the most or least attention—from polarizing bots and bullshit to boobs and borderline content.

4

Boobs and Borderline Content

"You can't take something off the Internet. That's like trying to take pee out of a swimming pool. Once it's in there, it's in there."

– Joe Garrelli, NewsRadio.

Most agree that limiting infodemics, misinformation and fake news is beneficial to public debate. This is easier said than done on social platforms: There is a lot of grey zone content detrimental to human health and well-being and disturbing democracy. From self-harm to sexualized content, to outright lies—what we're dealing with here is content that balances between the permissible and impermissible, depending on the community standards of the platform and the rule of law of the country in question.

Should the SoMe community be allowed to see hunger strikes, suicide letters, self-harm, animal cruelty or tween girls with duckfaces and fish gaps poses? And what about bare breasts, "dick pics" and other forms of sexualized imagery? Answers to such questions turn out to shape predominant historical narratives, public perception and cultural

© The Author(s), under exclusive license to Springer Nature
Switzerland AG 2022
V. F. Hendricks, C. Mehlsen, *The Ministry of Truth*,
https://doi.org/10.1007/978-3-030-98629-2_4

heritage that we as a society coalesce around. These are yet again—and to an ever greater extent—determined by the editorial practices, rules, regulations and automated algorithms of private platforms.

4.1   The Market for Nudes

If it weren't for porn, VHS would likely not have won the video war over Betamax and other video formats in the 1980s. And if it wasn't for sexually laden content, the Internet would probably not have broken through so quickly in the 1990s. In light hereof, it is not surprising that sharing nudes became a widespread phenomenon once social platforms and cell phones found their way into the everyday lives of billions of people in the twenty-first century.

As it became increasingly easy to share intimate pictures, a digital marketplace for naked photos and videos ('nudes') saw the light of day complete with buyers, sellers, brokers, goods and various forms of currency. This marketplace functions according to the well-known mechanisms governing markets as such *supply and demand*. If there is considerable demand for a naked photo of someone but such a photo is hard to come by, the item becomes sought after and in high demand. It can, for example, be a photo of an acclaimed actor in an intimate situation or a photo of a popular student from the neighboring school.

In this marketplace money is not necessarily the preferred currency for obtaining the item so persistently sought after. In the deep corners of the Internet exist subterranean trade-based economy for the exchange of nude photos. The entrance ticket to the closed "club" is the ability to hack one's way to illegal material. This sort of trading is comparable to trading sports car cards or Pokémon cards, but instead of a well-tuned Ferrari or turbo-charged Porsche, the "card" is of a (potentially famous) person photographed in an intimate situation. Hackers operate like collectors, who compare their "collections" with each other and then agree to swap one photo for another. This fuels an incentive to obtain new material, which they may then use to trade their way to an ever more valuable collection.[1]

It is not just in the dark deeps of the Internet where the trading of nudes is taking place. They are also exchanged and sold on major social platforms, although nudes and porn are strictly prohibited on the sites in question. Snapchat, Instagram, YouTube, Omegle and Discord are but some of the platforms used for distributing sexualized photos and videos, including content of minors, which is illegal globally. Social platforms remove millions of images and videos containing child nudity and exploitation every year, and numbers are rising: Several platforms, including Facebook, Instagram, Snapchat, and TikTok, have removed more 'child sexual abuse materials' (CSAM) in 2021 than in 2020.[2]

In a Danish documentary on TV2 ECHO 'For sale on Snapchat' from 2020, it was revealed that girls down to 14 years old use Snapchat to sell sexualized images and videos.[3] A 14 year old girl told TV2 that she sent photos of her butt and breasts to strangers on Snapchat. She was paid via a mobile payment app and then used the money to buy clothes and candy. Children's services and NGO's routinely receive

---

[1] Hopper, B. (2014). 'Inside the strange and seedy world where hackers trade celebrity nudes', The Verge, 04.09.2014, verified den 23.07.2021: https://www.theverge.com/2014/9/4/6106363/celebgate-fappening-naked-nude-celebrities-hack-hackers-trade

[2] Bischoff, P. (2022). 'The rising tide of child abuse content on social media', Comparitech.com 01.11.2022, verified 01.27.22: https://www.comparitech.com/blog/vpn-privacy/child-abuse-online-statistics/

[3] Mikkelsen, A.U. et al. (2020). 'Piger ned til 14 år sælger porno og sex på Snapchat – de nemme penge er fristende', TV2.dk, 03.08.2020, verified 23.07.2021: https://nyheder.tv2.dk/samfund/2020-08-03-piger-ned-til-14-aar-saelger-porno-og-sex-paa-snapchat-de-emme-penge-er

inquiries from young children and teenagers who find themselves involved in the digital market of buying and selling nudes. A 15 year old girl wrote to a hotline help service asking, "I sometimes send nudes to older people — is it illegal for me to receive money for it? People add my Snap, then I send them nudes in exchange for money."[4]

When nudes are sold and purchased on platforms, platforms in turn come to operate as involuntary middlemen, or fixers, connecting the buyers and sellers of sexualized content and services. This is a far cry from the original intent of the Internet as a free democratic harm free forum, a presumed pretense from which many first-mover social platforms back then was born.

Bare breasts, "dick pics" and other forms of nudes are genuine headaches for social platforms. The social platform Reddit's role in the so-called CelebGate-scandal serves as an example: When Kirsten Dunst, Jennifer Lawrence and 100 other celebrities turned on their screens in the days after September 1, 2014, they saw their private life displayed on the Internet. A hacker had leaked stolen nudes and videos of them on the social platform 4chang, after which they spread like wildfire into all the nooks and crannies of the web. In the days that followed, Reddit became one of the most popular distribution sites for stolen nudes. Reddit has, since its inception in 2005, been known as an open online forum where users (known as 'redditors') may share content and links on all sort of topics from gossip, humor and hobbies, to politics, science and news. Reddit stems from "the wisdom of the crowds" idea complete with a vision of being an open and

[4] Mehlsen, C. (2021). '8 ting du (måske) ikke vidste om unge og sexting', KommunikationsForum.dk, 16.06.2021, verified 23.07.2021: https://www.kommunikationsforum.dk/artikler/Boerns-Vilkaar-forklarer-sexting

democratic forum for opinions.[5] With more than 330 million active monthly users in 2021 Reddit is one of the most popular social platforms, especially among younger media users.[6]

In the first decade of the platform's lifetime, Reddit had a very liberal "hands free" approach to user content, that is, they did not want to control what users did or said on Reddit. This approach, however, was short-lived with the sudden appearance of stolen photos of naked celebrities on a Reddit subgroup, or 'subreddit', called TheFappening. TheFappening, which quickly became the unofficial distribution hotspot for hacked nudes brought such an enormous amount of traffic to the platform that at times it didn't operate properly. As a spokesperson for Reddit, Jason Harvey, wrote on Reddit on September 7, 2014:

> We hit new traffic milestones, ones which I'd be ashamed to share publicly.[7]

The Fappening put Reddit precisely between the rock and a hard place facing the dilemma social platforms time and again find themselves in: "*Should it stay or should it go?*". Should Reddit allow the prohibited content to remain on the platform and continue to believe in a "hands-free" approach? Or should Reddit intervene and drop the offending content and groups right off the platform? During 2010s social platforms were hardly sanctioned nudes, even if they broke the law. The inflicting material remained on sites; a problem which is far from resolved in the 2020s.

---

[5] Statista (2021). 'Reddit - Statistics & Facts'. 25.02.2021, verified 22.07.21: https://www.statista.com/topics/5672/reddit/

[6] Statista (2021). 'Reddit - Statistics & Facts'. 25.02.2021, verified 22.07.21: https://www.statista.com/topics/5672/reddit/

[7] Harvey, J. (2014). 'Time to talk', Reddit, 07.09.14, verified 22.07.2021: https://www.reddit.com/r/announcements/comments/2fpdax/time_to_talk/

Given a few days Reddit decided to shut down TheFappening and other related subreddits. A couple of months after TheFappening was shut down, Ellen Pao became the acting CEO of Reddit. She had been employed at the company since 2013 and was an integral part of the company leadership when the stolen celebrity nudes gave Reddit what platforms of the information age live of—traffic numbers. One of the first initiatives initiated with Pao at the helm in 2015, was to ban the sharing of nudes without consent. As Pao said in an interview years later:

> When I became CEO, one of the first things we did was to ban revenge porn and unauthorized nude photos and it ended up that we were the first major platform to do that. Then all of the other platforms followed (…) I think they were waiting for somebody to take the first step, and we were the ones who ended up doing it.[8]

In May 2015, Reddit took further action and closed several hate speech groups and other groups featuring abusive content directed at individuals. The platform thereby challenged the role of self-appointed moderators, who are otherwise tasked with keeping tabs on the many different fora on the platform. As Reddit explained in it's own subgroup June 10, 2015:

> We will ban subreddits that allow their communities to use the subreddit as a platform to harass individuals when moderators don't take action. We're banning behavior, not ideas.[9]

---

[8] Ellen Pao in interview with Camilla Mehlsen, Mountain View, California, 29.05.2019.

[9] u/reddit (2015): 'Removing harassing subreddits', 10.07.2015, verified 22.07.2021:

https://www.reddit.com/r/announcements/comments/39bpam/removing_harassing_subreddits/

Pao received harsh criticism from a large army of Reddit users and moderators strongly disagreeing with the decision to remove content and shut down discussion groups—and who accused Pao of impinging on freedom of speech. She received hate mail, death threats and threats to share her private information, which Pao described as "one of the largest trolling attacks in history.[10] After the massive criticism and disagreement between the leaders of Reddit's growth planners, Pao stepped down as CEO in the summer of 2015 and has since established the non-profit organization Project Include, which advises tech companies on diversity and inclusion.

Pao spoke out, in an interview in 2019, saying that it would be denying freedom of expression if a platform and its users didn't take up the fight against hate speech and other forms of abusive content intended to violate people and their privacy, such as sharing nudes:

> The purpose of free speech is to have the sharing of ideas and to make sure that you have everybody being able to express their ideas. When the speech used is not really sharing that idea but really just intended to push people off a platform, you are, by banning it, not scrubbing free speech, you are encouraging free speech. You are encouraging everybody to be able to participate. Otherwise you end up where only the loud voices remain and that is not free speech. It is just the loudest person or the meanest person trying to say horrible things to push other people off the platform. That is not a public square to use.[11]

---

[10] Pao, E. (2015). 'The trolls are winning the battle for the Internet', *The Washington Post*, 16.07.2015, verified 03.08.21: https://www.washingtonpost.com/opinions/we-cannot-let-the-internet-trolls-win/2015/07/16/91b1a2d2-2b17-11e5-bd33-395c05608059_story.html

[11] Ellen Pao in interview with Camilla Mehlsen, Mountain View, California, 29.05.2019.

Here Paos' ideas concur with the visions of John Perry Barlow and John Stuart Mill, presented in the first chapter. The marketplace of free ideas and public space can lose its value if one is able to systematically suppress the free ideas of others, or force others to shy away from public life through shaming, extortion or threats of retaliation because of their mere presence, specific act or other privileges enjoyed. In such a scenario there is no level playing field. Only the loudest voices prevail.

4.2   Edgy Content

Shortly after her exit from Reddit, Ellen Pao wrote a column, in *The Washington* Post, arguing that the forefathers of the Internet were plainly naïve to believe in open information sharing. They believed in 'the good' but in reality the Internet, including Reddit, is composed of "The good, the bad and the ugly" (also the title of Sergio Leone's 1966 classic Western movie).[12] Users tend to flock to boundary pushing content while the behavior of extremist users pivot between the bad and the ugly. If a social platform wants to reach a broad public audience and attract the largest advertisers, the platform needs to remove "the ugly" such as harassment, suicide and child pornography, and take greater responsibility for objectionable content such as lies and hate speech. However, social platforms struggle to define the right divide between "the bad" and "the ugly".

Facebook's founder and CEO, Mark Zuckerberg, delved into the dilemma of finding the right divide and strike a

---

[12] Pao, E. (2015). 'The trolls are winning the battle for the Internet', *The Washington Post*, 16.07.2015, verified 03.08.21: https://www.washingtonpost.com/opinions/we-cannot-let-the-internet-trolls-win/2015/07/16/91b1a2d2-2b17-11e5-bd33-395c05608059_story.html

balance in "A Blueprint for Content Governance and Enforcement" in 2018. The blueprint described how users are attracted to all forms of boundary pushing content, even if they don't acknowledge it themselves. As Zuckerberg writes:

> Our research suggests that no matter where we draw the lines for what is allowed, as a piece of content gets close to that line, people will engage with it more on average — even when they tell us afterwards they don't like the content.[13]

Sexualized photos, misinformation, hate speech, self-harm and clickbait are examples of content categories that belong to what social platforms label 'borderline content' or in other words, boundary breaking content at the limit of what platforms allow. While established media adhere to the press' rule of ethics and journalistic codes of conduct, the edgy content in question typically isn't considered illegal around the world. Borderline content may also be harmful content, such as self-harm, suicide or hate speech which can have an adverse infectious effect on fellow users. Zuckerberg explains:

> Interestingly, our research has found that this natural pattern of borderline content getting more engagement, applies not only to news but to almost every category of content. For example, photos close to the line of nudity, like with revealing clothing or sexually suggestive positions, got more engagement on average before we changed the distribution curve to discourage this.[14]

---

[13] Zuckerberg, M. (2018). 'A Blueprint for Content Governance and Enforcement', verified 03.08.2021: https://m.facebook.com/nt/screen/?params=%7B%22note_id%22%3A751449002072082%7D&path=%2Fnotes%2Fnote%2F&refsrc=deprecated&_rdr

[14] Zuckerberg, M. (2018). 'A Blueprint for Content Governance and Enforcement', verified 03.08.2021: https://m.facebook.com/nt/screen/?params=%7B%22note_id%22%3A751449002072082%7D&path=%2Fnotes%2Fnote%2F&refsrc=deprecated&_rdr

According to Zuckerberg, the solution isn't to remove borderline content but to reduce its visibility. Or as he formulates it: Facebook and Instagram "punish borderline content so it gets less distribution and engagement." This editorial strategy is known as shadow banning. Facebook for instance changed the algorithms for newsfeeds such that content that comes close to violating the platform's content policy reaches fewer users (Fig. 4.1). The boundary for when content is considered 'borderline' and harmful is constantly changing as platforms face new problems pertaining to user content. In the summer of 2019, Zuckerberg & Co. was confronted with this dilemma: How should Instagram respond to a suicide note posted by an influencer with thousands of young followers? *Should it stay or should it go?* Is a suicide note a cry for help that may save a life? Will it have a contagious effect on young people? The answer to both questions may very well be "yes".

A 23 year old Danish influencer and reality TV personality posted a suicide note on her Instagram profile and thus to more than 330.000 young followers. In the note she told her family, friends and followers about difficulties in life and the downside of being famous, her final words being that she now wanted to fly up to heavens to meet her grandfather. Her post immediately got thousands of likes and comments, most of them supporting the influencer, albeit there were also comments from young people sharing their own suicidal thoughts. The post was reported to Instagram but the platform didn't remove it because "it does not violate our Community Guidelines," the platform concluded. The influencer's family wanted to remove the post but couldn't do so. The note, however, was also a blessing: The young girl was found a few hours after publishing the post, brought to the hospital and fortunately she survived. Two days after publishing the post she removed it from Instagram.

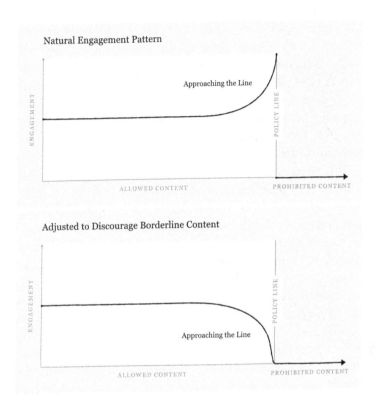

Fig. 4.1 The more provoking and forbidden content is, the more engagement it receives—unless the platform changes the distribution curve, so borderline content, which is close to violating the platform's guidelines, is distributed to fewer users. Source: Facebook (Zuckerberg, M. (2018). 'A Blueprint for Content Governance and Enforcement', verified 03.08.2021: https://m.facebook.com/nt/screen/?params=%7B%22note_id%22%3A751449002072082%7D&path=%2Fnotes%2Fnote%2F&refsrc=deprecated&_rdr)

According to World Health Organization, suicide is the fourth leading cause of death among 15–19 year old teenagers around the globe.[15] When a British 14 year old girl took her own life in her bedroom, it later came to light that she

[15] WHO (2021). "Suicide", 17.06.2021, verified 27.01.2022: https://www.who.int/news-room/fact-sheets/detail/suicide

had been exposed to self-harm content and networks on Instagram. Instagram received massive criticism for not doing enough to protect vulnerable users from harmful content. Afterwards Facebook tightened its content policy. Users were no longer allowed to share photos of open sores and the company made it more difficult to search for self-harm material and profiles on its platforms, e.g. by hiding posts for #selfharm and #suicide.[16]

This is yet another example of Facebook recognizing that content may have harmful and contagious effects on other users and that the platform not only has a responsibility but simultaneously decides where and how the lines are drawn.

According to whistleblower Francis Haugen, Instagram doesn't react in responsible manner in order to protect its young users: In the *Facebook Files* leaked in September 2021, an internal study showed that Instagram has harmful effects on teenagers, especially girls.[17] One negative impact is on young users with suicidal thoughts: 13% of British users, and 6% of American teen users, trace the desire to commit suicide to Instagram. Another disturbing finding from the leaked files is that every third teen girl report that when they feel bad about their bodies, Instagram make them feel even worse. Or as reported in an internal presentation: "We make body image issues worse for one in three teen girls."[18]

---

[16] Reuters (2019). "Facebook and Instagram tighten rules on self-harm images", 10.09.2019, verified 09.08.2021: https://www.reuters.com/article/us-facebook-content-idUSKCN1VV1XT

[17] *Wall Street Journal* (2021). *The Facebook Files*, verified 29.01.2022: https://www.wsj.com/articles/the-facebook-files-11631713039.:

[18] Wall Street Journal (2021). "Facebook Knows Instagram is Toxic for Teen Girls, Company Documents Show", 14.09.2022, verified 29.01.2022: https://www.wsj.com/articles/facebook-knows-instagram-is-toxic-for-teen-girls-company-documents-show-11631620739

4.3   Activism or Eyewitnessing

When yet another conflict between Israel and Palestine broke out in the spring of 2021, it escalated to an armed confrontation including Israeli air strikes and rocket launches from Hamas, street fights between police forces and Palestinian demonstrators and sporadic private attacks amongst civilians. Throughout these events, which culminated in a ceasefire agreement between Israel and Hamas on May 20, 2021, ordinary citizens and the press made extensive use of social platforms to report on violent incidents and on conditions in the warzone. At the al-Aqsa Mosque in Jerusalem in particular, where fierce fighting broke out between Israeli police and Palestinians, many on Instagram used the hashtag #AlAqsa to bring attention to the fighting. But Instagram's algorithm-based moderation architecture instead removed content with the #AlAqsa hashtag and hid it from searches. The reason was supposedly that Facebook, which owns Instagram, had categorized "alaqsa" as "dangerous individuals or organizations." (Fig. 4.2)[19]

A group of employees at Instagram repeatedly called attention to the fact that users could not see pro-Palestinian content during the conflict. Perhaps it was by mistake, but as an employee at Instagram pointed out (Fig. 4.3): "… moderating at scale is biased against any marginalized groups."[20]

---

[19] Mac, R. (2021). "Instagram Censored Posts About One Of Islam's Holiest Mosques, Drawing Employee Ire", *BuzzFeed*, 12.05.2021, verified 06.06.2021:   https://www.buzzfeednews.com/article/ryanmac/instagram-facebook-censored-al-aqsa-mosque

[20] Lyons, K. (2021). "Instagram making changes to its algorithm after it was accused of censoring pro-Palestinian content", *The Verge*, 30.05.2021, verified 06.06.2021:https://www.theverge.com/2021/5/30/22460946/instagram-making-changes-algorithm-censoring-pro-palestinian-content

Fig. 4.2   Instagram initially removed material related to #AlAqsa

This bias in Instagram's content moderation was, among other things, discussed on Twitter which also came under fire during the conflict. The Palestinian-American author Mariam Barghouti reported from the ground about protests over forcing Palestinians from their homes in the Sheikh Jarrah neighborhood in East Jerusalem (Fig. 4.4). Immediately thereafter, her Twitter account was temporarily suspended with a message that her profile broke Twitter's media policy. The first section of Twitter's media policy for "sensitive content" reads:

> You may not post media that is excessively gory or share violent or adult content within live video or in profile header, or List banner images. Media depicting sexual violence and/or assault is also not permitted.[21]

However, none of Barghooti's tweets about the conflict seemed to violate the guidelines. Twitter has since recognized

---

[21] Twitter: Sensitive Media Policy (2021): https://help.twitter.com/en/rules-and-policies/media-policy

Fig. 4.3 Twitter post on Instagram's moderation practice during the Israeli-Palestinian conflict, May 2021

that the temporary suspension was a mistake without specifying how or why the mistake happened.[22]

[22] Maiberg, E. (2021). "Twitter Said It Restricted Palestinian Writer's Account by Accident", *Vice*, 12.05.2021, verified 06.06.2021:

https://www.vice.com/en/article/qj8b4x/twitter-said-it-restricted-palestinian-writers-account-by-accident

Fig. 4.4 Mariam Berghouti's tweet that prompted Twitter to temporarily suspend her account

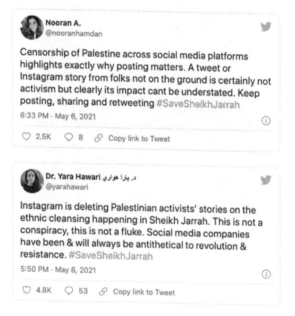

Fig. 4.5 Eyewitness accounts or activism?

Instagram's and Twitter's indecisiveness is likely due to the fact that content moderation must weigh whether posts like these have the character of eye witness accounts "from staff on assignment" or are closer to a form of activism that may lead to further uprisings (Fig. 4.5). If a tweet encourages unrest or violence it can actually violate the platform's guidelines. However, if it is the former of the two, then it is indeed central to the platform's *raison d'être*. During the Arab Spring in 2010–2011 social platforms played a significant role in the popular protests against the regimes of a number of Arabic countries. With this new form of digital mobilization it became clear how social platforms could give citizens around the world a voice and access to information both otherwise often in short supply.

Social platforms give individual citizens the opportunity to proclaim and defend their cause, but they also give governments the potential to control the information flow to the public. In September 2016, a delegation from Facebook held a meeting with then Israeli Justice Minister, Ayelet Shaked, and Security Minister Gilad Erdan with the aim of improving "cooperation against incitement to terror and murder", as it was called in a press release from then Prime Minister Benjamin Natanyahu's office.[23] The year after, the Israeli Ministry of Justice released a report from its cyber unit showing that it had handled 2.241 cases of online content and removed 70% of the material in question.[24] Facebook also "works very closely with cyber units in the Ministry of Justice, the police, and with other elements in the army and Shin Bet," according to an interview with Facebook's country manager of Israel from 2017.[25]

It is an exceedingly difficult balance to give a voice to eyewitness accounts and to the opinions of users who want to be

---

[23] Gostoli, Y. (2018). "Palestinians fight Facebook, YouTube censorship", Aljazeera. com, 20.01.2018, verified 06.06.2021: https://www.aljazeera.com/ news/2018/1/20/palestinians-fight-facebook-youtube-censorship

[24] State Attorney (2017). Report 04.07–2017, verified 30.01.2022: https://www. justice.gov.il/Units/StateAttorney/Publications/OnTheAgenda/Pages/04-07-17-05.aspx

[25] Calcalist (2017). *Interview: Jordana Cutler, Calcalist*, 17.12.2017, verified 06.06.2021: https://www.calcalist.co.il/local/articles/0,7340,L-3728279,00.html

activists, but at the same time not activistic in a way that incites violence and hatred.

And what about the denial of murder and violence? How should the platforms for example respond to Holocaust denials? Until October 2020 Mark Zuckerberg's position was that social platforms should not remove Holocaust denials. As he said in an interview with tech journalist Kara Swisher in 2018:

> I'm Jewish, and there's a set of people who deny that the Holocaust happened. I find that deeply offensive. But at the end of the day, I don't believe that our platform should take that down because I think there are things that different people get wrong.[26]

A short time after, Mark Zuckerberg, in an email to Kara Swisher, continued that, in his interview with her, he wasn't trying to defend the intention of Holocaust deniers. At the same time he stressed that the platform's goal with fake news was not to stop people from saying untrue things but to stop fake news and misinformation from spreading on Facebook's services.[27]

The tune changed a couple of years later when Facebook decided to forbid all content that denied or distorted the Holocaust. Facebook chose to update its policy for hate speech after an increase in anti-Semitism, both online and offline. Mark Zuckerberg announced the decision on his own Facebook profile on October 12, 2020, where he

---

[26] Swisher, K. (2018). "Zuckerberg: The Recode Interview", *Vox*, 8.10.2018, verified 13.06.2021: https://www.vox.com/2018/7/18/17575156/mark-zuckerberg-interview-facebook-recode-kara-swisher

[27] Swisher, K. (2018). "Mark Zuckerberg clarifies: 'I personally find holocaust denial deeply offensive, and I absolutely didn't intend to defend the intent of people who deny it", *Vox*, 18.07.2018, verified 13.06.2021: https://www.vox.com/2018/7/18/17588116/mark-zuckerberg-clarifies-holocaust-denial-offensive

"I've struggled with the tension between standing for free expression and the harm caused by minimizing or denying the horror of the Holocaust. My own thinking has evolved as I've seen data showing an increase in anti-Semitic violence, as have our wider policies on hate speech. Drawing the right lines between what is and isn't acceptable speech isn't straightforward, but with the current state of the world, I believe this is the right balance."

Fig. 4.6 Mark Zuckerberg's announcement that he's tightening the grip on Holocaust denial on Facebook (Zuckerberg, M. 2020. Facebook, 12.10.2020, verified 25.06.2021: https://www.facebook.com/zuck/posts/10112455086578451)

explained that his attitude changed after he became aware of data that showed a rise in anti-Semitic violence (Fig. 4.6).

The decision to remove Holocaust denials happened immediately after Facebook also decided to remove profiles, sites or groups that represented the conspiracy theory QAnon, even if the content didn't directly reference violence or hate. This signaled the end of claims that politicians, Hollywood stars and journalists were part of an elite satanic pedophile ring behind coronavirus as an instrument to control the world.[28]

Since his interview with Kara Swisher in 2018 Mark Zuckerberg has refused to do another interview with her. The very first question Kara Swisher would like to ask him though, is also one that most urgently needs an answer:

Why tell everyone that you do not want to be an arbiter of truth after you purposefully built a platform that absolutely required an arbiter of truth to function properly?[29]

---

[28] Facebook (2020). "An Update to How We Address Movements and Organizations Tied to Violence", *Facebook*, 19.08.2020, verified 14.06.2021: https://about.fb.com/news/2020/08/addressing-movements-and-organizations-tied-to-violence/

[29] Swisher, K. (2020). "Mark Zuckerberg's 'Evolving' Position on Holocaust Denial", *The New York Times*, 14.10.2020, verified 13.06.2021: https://www.nytimes.com/2020/10/14/opinion/facebook-holocaust-denial.html

Facebook says it doesn't want to be the arbiter of truth but this is exactly the role it inadvertently holds when the platform makes editorial decisions about what is true and false, which material is granted attention and which content is suppressed — and what is historically significant.

4.4   Napalm Girl Caught in the Net

Some photos are so powerful they can change our understanding of world events. However, it is usually only in retrospect we get to know which photos come to encapsulate significant moments in history. This is evidenced by the Vietnam War's most iconic image:

1972: A flock of burned children run crying from a violent attack of napalm bombs in Vietnam. Central in the photo is 9 year old Kim Phúc. She was naked because she had removed her burning clothes of the napalm fire. When photographer Nick Ut snapped the photo later entitled *The Terror of War*, better known as the "Napalm girl", for the Associated Press in 1972, the Vietnam War's gruesome consequences became clear for the rest of the world. The image had a transformational impact on the public perception of the War. The girl's pain was a contributing factor to the public's growing opposition to the Vietnam War and to winding down the war. The photograph earned Nick Ut a Pulitzer Prize in 1973 and has become one of the world's most iconic wartime photos (Fig. 4.7).[30]

2016: 44 years after the bombing, the Napalm girl image initiated an entirely different form of resistance—one that would define a turning point for Facebook. The Norwegian

---

[30] The Pulitzer Prizes (2021). "The Terror of War", The 1973 Pulitzer Prize Winner in Spot News Photography, verified 03.08.2021: https://www.pulitzer.org/winners/huynh-cong-ut

Fig. 4.7   **Terror of War** is the Vietnam War's most iconic photo, 1972

author Tom Egelund shared an article on Facebook about seven images that had changed the history of warfare. One of the seven photos was the Napalm girl but, since the girl was naked, it blatantly violated Facebook's community standards and Facebook removed the photo from Tom Egelund's profile. When Tom Egelund voiced his criticism of this decision on his Facebook profile his account was placed in temporary quarantine: His profile was closed down for 24 h, during which he was unable to post content on Facebook.[31]

Facebook's actions invoked considerable ire from journalists, politicians and other Facebook users. The Norwegian newspaper *Aftenposten* also received a message that it should remove the photos of the naked girl from it's official Facebook profile. This prompted the newspaper, on September 9,

[31] Wong, J.C. (2016)." Mark Zuckerberg accused of abusing power after Facebook deletes 'napalm girl' post", *The Guardian*, 09.09.2016, verified 03.08.2021: https://www.theguardian.com/technology/2016/sep/08/facebook-mark-zuckerberg-napalm-girl-photo-vietnam-war

2016, to update its front page with a letter to Facebook's founder Mark Zuckerberg:

> Dear Mark Zuckerberg, I follow you on Facebook, but you don't know me. I am editor-in-chief of the Norwegian daily newspaper Aftenposten. I am writing this letter to inform you that I shall not comply with your requirement to remove a documentary photography [sic] from the Vietnam War made by Nick Ut.

In the letter, the newspaper's chief editor, Espen Egil-Hansen, explained why the Napalm girl held significant historical value.

> The Napalm girl is by far the most iconic documentary photography from the Vietnam war. The media played a decisive role in reporting different stories about the war than the men in charge wanted them to publish. They brought about a change of attitude which played a role in ending the war. They contributed to a more open, more critical debate. This is how a democracy must function.[32]

Aftenposten's criticism went viral on social media and thousands of Facebook user's began to protest, in a sort of intra-Facebook act of civil disobedience, by posting pictures of the iconic image on their own profiles. One of them was the then prime minister of Norway, Erna Solberg, who herself had the image removed from her Facebook profile and afterwards declared: "What they achieve by removing such images, good as the intentions may be, is to edit our common history."[33]

---

[32] Hansen, E.E. (2016). "Dear Mark. I am writing this to inform you that I shall not comply with your requirement to remove this picture", *Aftenposten*, 08.09.2016, verified 04.08.2021: https://www.aftenposten.no/meninger/kommentar/i/G892Q/dear-mark-i-am-writing-this-to-inform-you-that-i-shall-not-comply-wit

[33] Kjærgaard Larsen, L. (2016). "Flere kritiserer Facebook for at fjerne billede fra Vietnam-krigen", Dr.dk, 09.09.2016, verified 15.08.2021: https://www.dr.dk/ligetil/flere-kritiserer-facebook-fjerne-billede-fra-vietnam-krigen

At Facebook the protest was a turning point. The platform, which otherwise systematically removed naked images, changed its stance and allowed the image of the Napalm girl to remain.

The protests shed light on the dilemma that social platforms, like Facebook, Instagram, Twitter, YouTube and LinkedIn, find themselves in: Because of their size they have control over the words, images, videos and soundbites that billions of people see, hear and listen to. But what happens if the next image, with the potential to change worldviews or public opinion, infringes on the platforms' community rules, so that it is removed or its visibility dialed down before it even gains attention?

What now, if the 3 year old boy Aylan Kurdi had been naked or had a large open wound in his head when he lay lifeless on the beach with his face buried in the sand in Turkey (Fig. 4.8)? Would the dead Syrian refugee be "*persona non grata*" of the social platforms? This wasn't the case in 2015: A short time after Aylan Kurdis' body was found on the Turkish beach, heart-wrenching images spread from a Turkish news agency to social platforms with hashtags such as #kiyiyaVuranInsanlik (Turkish for "humanity washed ashore"), #DrownedSyrianBoy og #SyriaCrisis.

Within 12 h, photos of the dead Syrian boy had spread to over 20 million people around the world.[34] The pictures of the boy led to an intense debate about Europe's responsibility towards refugees. An example of how this effectuated a change in attitude could be seen in the tone of the language used on Twitter when referencing immigration: In the period after the images went viral, the word "refugee" became more widespread than "migrant" (Figs. 4.8 and 4.9).

---

[34] The University of Sheffield (2015). "Aylan Kurdi: How a single image transformed the debate on immigration", 14.12.2015, verified 09.08.2021: https://www.sheffield.ac.uk/news/nr/aylan-kurdi-social-media-report-1.533951

Fig. 4.8 Three year old Aylan Kurdi's dead body washed ashore on a beach in Turkey, 2015

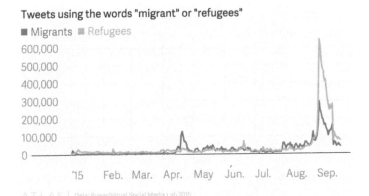

Tweets using the words "migrant" or "refugees"

■ Migrants ■ Refugees

Fig. 4.9 Testimony that the word refugee is used more often than migrant on Twitter in 2015. Source: Pulsar/Visual Social Media Lab, 2015

Even though the images of Aylan Kurdi were at the very limit of what the established media and television normally would publish or broadcast, many chose to publish anyway. *The Los Angeles Times* published one of the more disturbing images, namely a close-up of the boy, reasoning that a single image could change the story:

> The image is not offensive, it is not gory or tasteless — it is merely heartbreaking and a stark testimony of an unfolding human tragedy that is playing out in Syria, Turkey and Europe, often unwitnessed. (...) It took [a picture of] a tiny boy on a beach to finally reach those who may not yet have understood the extent of the crisis.[35]

4.5   The Custodians of History

The image of a burned Kim Phúc in Vietnam and the image of dead Aylan Kurdi in Turkey are both stark visual testimonies. In time, they become part of our shared history and shared memory. Strong images can help focus attention, form public opinion and steer language use and global views. With social platforms and the information driven infrastructure of the digital age, these types of images may spread further and faster than ever before. It can well be that the public memory is short, but the web never forgets. For most users, the web represents an easily accessible and searchable repository of historical events, periods and zeitgeists. It is part of our common historical consciousness and an integral part of the cultural heritage of good and evil.

---

[35] Los Angeles Times (2015). "Editorial: The death of Aylan Kurdi and the need for a moral policy on refugees", *Los Angeles Times*, 03.09.2015, verified 03.08.2021: https://www.latimes.com/opinion/editorials/la-ed-migrants-20150904-story.html

Social platforms play a part in writing history when the sheer mention of a person is forbidden on a given platform. This was the case with the British right wing activist Tommy Robinson, whose Facebook profile with over a million followers in 2019 was not only blocked; fellow users also had their content blocked if they just mentioned his name. In George Orwell's *1984* one can risk being a "non-person," that is written out of history. In the novel the Party refers to the proverb:

Who controls the past controls the future. Who controls the present controls the past. (Orwell 1949): 156

If we aren't sober and careful here and now, we may very well end up in a situation where social platforms and search engines dominate present day information and further down the line can control future stories about what is the present and as of right! now! is the past. If one controls access to information spaces, the infrastructure of the digital public sphere, including their content, both the present and the past may to significant extent be mastered—and remastered. It is on present information that we contemplate future decisions and actions, as well as rationalize, reminisce and reflect upon what transpired in the past.

To be the arbiter of truth means not only to be the master of what is true or false, what is misinformation, fake news or bullshit, but also to decide upon the context—whether historical, artistic, activistic, or satirical—of a particular piece of content as well as the underlying rationale for setting it into circulation. If some snippet of content appears or may be interpreted as irony or satire in a given context, then there should be room for it, but if the context on the other hand is interpreted as promoting hate or violence then it shouldn't have a place. As a tech platform, while determining whether some piece of content should be allowed, you are willingly or unwillingly also in the business of context interpretation and determination of motive. While the goal of intent is to act and set the content into circulation, the motive decides the reasoning behind an action or post. But intent and motive may be functions of both context and content in circulation, as it is often only the latter which is available while having to weighing in on whether to allow a particular piece of material to gain traction and attention.

When social platforms are suddenly given such prominent and powerful roles and act as *de facto* custodians and curators of public memory and cultural heritage, it means that their community standards, terms of usage and editorial rules easily become integral parts of historiography—and that's never without bias as American professor of media, former director of MIT Center for Civic Media and Internet activist, Ethan Zuckerman, pointedly notes:

> Curators are great, but they're inherently biased. Curators are always making an editorial decision. Those biases have really big implications.[36]

The platforms themselves are actually the gatekeepers and the ones who get to choose which words, images, stories and profiles deserve attention. Is the SoMe population and broader public allowed to see hunger strikes, suicide letters, self-harm, animal abuse, man breasts or scantily dressed tweens with duckfaces? These are the questions whose answers create the narratives of history and form the cultural inheritance that we as a society gather around, but which now become functions of privatized editorial practices and

[36] Scharfenberg, D. (2013). "MIT's Zuckerman On Building A More Cosmopolitan Internet", *wbur*, 17.07.2013, verified 29.01.2022: https://www.wbur.org/news/2013/07/17/zuckerman-rewire-interview

automated algorithm architectures. Platforms and search engines are now actively taking part in writing history, whether we or they like it or not. And if in doubt about the course of history, it is rarely the national archives or the library that we frequent first. We just Google it.

5

Influencers and Superspreaders

"Influencers – they're the best thing since sliced bread. But forget bread. They're selling like hot cakes. They're creating huge returns, and they're only set to keep growing!"

– Emily Warna

A new kind of agent has emerged on the attention economy stage—*the influencer*. Profiles with many followers act as nodes in social networks and can move markets and agendas. Influencers are the top 1% in the attention economy. Each and every day influencers reach billions of people on a host of different topics, ranging from fashion, travel, health, diets and exercise to sports, gaming, activism, politics and many other agenda items.

In the slipstream of the Covid-19 pandemic it has become evident that influencers and other large profiles act as superspreaders in networks that can set and proliferate, from misinformed to well-informed and knowledgeable agendas to the public as well as established media.

The impact of influencers on people and public sphere is intimately connected to social platforms, which in the final

© The Author(s), under exclusive license to Springer Nature Switzerland AG 2022
V. F. Hendricks, C. Mehlsen, *The Ministry of Truth*,
https://doi.org/10.1007/978-3-030-98629-2_5

analysis hold the power over influencer bullhorns. Remove the bullhorn and abracadabra… the influencers disappear.

5.1   The Power of Influence

On June 21st 2021, during the UEFA European Football Championship, Portuguese footballer Cristiano Ronaldo received massive attention for a gesture lasting only a few seconds, followed by a single word—and it wasn't about soccer. During the pregame press conference between Portugal and Hungary, Ronaldo removed the Coca-Cola bottles on the table, took his own water bottle in hand and with a preferential tone said "aqua".

The superstar is heavily invested in healthy lifestyle and signaled with a single word that he would rather drink water than soda. In the following days the clip went viral and several stories emerged in the media that Ronaldo's stunt had shaved four billion dollars off Coca-Colas' market value. It was later disclosed that Coca-Colas' stock had begun its downward slide before the press meeting took place, and that its massive loss could therefore not be directly attributed to Ronaldo's action. There is no doubt, however, that when a superstar such as Ronaldo communicates to the public, his millions of fans and followers listen.

Ronaldo has more than 350 million followers on Instagram alone and thereby enjoys pole position with most followers of any other personal profile on the platform (Fig. 5.1). The only other profile with more followers is Instagram's official profile with an excess of around 450 million followers. Ronaldo is known as one of the world's best soccer players, but on his Instagram profile he is an influencer who shares stories about being indeed a soccer player, about his private life (e.g. selfies with his son) and sponsored collaborations. By way of example, Ronaldo sermonizes about having a

1. Instagram: 441 million followers
2. Cristiano (Cristiano Ronaldo): 366 million followers
3. Kylie Jenner: 281 million followers
4. Lionel Messi: 281 million followers
5. The Rock (Dwayne 'The Rock' Johnson): 278 million followers

Fig. 5.1 The five largest Instagram profiles measured by number of followers according to *Brandwatch*, November 2021 (Boyd, J. (2021). "The Top 20 Most Followed Instagram Accounts". *Brandwatch*, 14.11.2021, verified 28.01.2022: https://www.brandwatch.com/blog/top-most-instagram-followers/). Instagram is one of the largest platforms for influencer marketing

positive mindset while promoting his collaboration with Nike. Ronaldo's role as an influencer is in one of the reasons he is the first soccer player with a billion dollar income. A single post on Ronaldo's profile can cost upwards of ten million dollars.[1]

Words represent power and capital when an influencer can move markets by simply using their outlets to either criticize or condone a product or business. Influencer, reality star and cosmetics entrepreneur, Kylie Jenner was able to give Snapchat a significant blow on Wall Street, with a single tweet. This happened on February 21st 2018, when she expressed her discontent with Snapchat's new design: "sooo does anyone else not open Snapchat anymore? Or is it just me ... ugh this is so sad."[2] Shortly after Snapchat's market value tanked 1.3 billion dollars.[3]

The highest YouTube earner in the world, 3 years in a row, was neither a soccer player nor a reality star, but a completely ordinary boy. Ryan Kaji, born in 2011, ranked No. 1 on

[1] Hopper HQ (2021). "Instagram Richlist", verified 15.08.2021: https://www.hopperhq.com/instagram-rich-list//#FullTable
[2] Kylie Jenner on Twitter 21.02.2018, verified 15.08.2021: https://twitter.com/KylieJenner/status/966429897118728192
[3] Vasquez, J. (2018). "In One Tweet, Kylie Jenner Wiped Out $1.3 Billion of Snap's Market Value", *Bloomberg*, 11.02.2018, verified 15.08.2021.

Forbes Magazine's list of the highest-paid YouTube stars in 2018–2020.[4] In 2020, he made $26 million on YouTube. His claim to fame is playing: He plays with, and reviews, toys on his YouTube channel *Ryan's World* and has additionally created his own line of toys. The most watched videos on Ryan's channel have more than a billion views. In it he uses the popular unboxing genre where toys either bought or gifted, are displayed for others to see. Ryan unboxes a gigantic egg from Disney, filled with Disney's *Cars* toys. Revenue is generated primarily from commercials on his channel but also from collaborations.

According to *Forbes Magazine*, Ryan Kaji dropped down to No. 7 on the list of the highest-paid YouTube stars in 2021, although the revenue of Ryan Kaji's channel had increased: He made $27 million in 2021 as a YouTuber. The sixth highest ranking YouTuber on Forbes list is the 7 year old Russian girl, Anastasia Radzinskaya, who has more than 100 million followers on her YouTube channel, Nastya, and $28 million in revenue in 2021. No 1 in 2021 is a 23 year old American man named MrBeast earning massive $54 million on his entertaining stunt-videos which earned 10 billion views during the year.[5]

An influencer is a person who produces original content on social media platforms (Instagram, YouTube, TikTok, etc.,) and/or blogs, for their many followers; they hold the power to exert influence on followers with their opinions, tastes and preferences (Mehlsen 2020). The term influencer is a catchall phrase for a content creator while platform

---

[4] Berg, M. & Brown, A. (2020). "The Highest-Paid YouTube Stars of 2020", *Forbes*, 18.12.2020, verified 15.08.2021: https://www.forbes.com/sites/maddieberg/2020/12/18/the-highest-paid-youtube-stars-of-2020/?sh=64edf1fc6e50

[5] Brown, A. & Freeman, A. (2022). "The Highest-Paid YouTube Stars: MrBeast, Jake Paul and Markplier Score Massive Paydays", *Forbes*, 22.1.2022, verified 28.1.2022: https://www.forbes.com/sites/abrambrown/2022/01/14/the-highest-paid-youtube-stars-mrbeast-jake-paul-and-markiplier-score-massive-paydays

specific terms for large profiles, such as 'YouTuber', 'Instagrammer' and 'TikToker,' reflect their outlet.

Anyone with a social platform profile is their own media outlet. An influencer's operations are merely markedly more vast in scope and often have commercial interest vested in their online presence. Influencers gain attention and, supposedly, recognition as an 'ordinary everyday person', making them recognizable and authentic in the eyes of their followers. Companies that pay influencers to advertise, not only get their products rubber stamped by the influencer, they also gain direct access to their network.

Even though an influencer is typically approachable for commercial collaboration, it is important to note that the sway of an influencer by far exceeds what may be measured in advertisement revenue. An influencer's online status is social capital that may be converted to other forms of capital (Mehlsen 2020). Social capital is often exchanged for monetary capital, where the influencer receives payment from a sponsoring company or organization, but social capital can also be traded for political or cultural capital. For example, reality star and influencer Kim Kardashian West was invited to the White House by former President Donald J. Trump in 2019 to discuss criminal justice reform, specifically the First Step Act. Trump subsequently voiced his support for the Act.[6]

In the attention economy it is of paramount importance to be heard—and some are heard far more than others. As French economist Thomas Piketty says, it's a bit like the World economy: The wealthiest 1% own 50% of the world's riches, while remaining 99% of the population must share the remaining 50%. Influencers are the attention economy's one-percenters.

---

[6] Fink, J. (2019). "Kim Kardashian West Thanks Donald Trump for Signing First Step Act Allowing Matthew Charles to Be Freed", *Newsweek*, 03.01.2019, verified 08.01.2022: https://www.newsweek.com/kim-kardashian-west-thanks-donald-trump-signing-first-step-act-allowing-1278881

From an attention economic perspective, influencers and other larger than life profiles are attention entrepreneurs (Wu 2016). They act as 'attention magnets' that attract likes, followers and engagement … and are in the end part and parcel in providing the valuable data fuel to the attention economy business model. The operations of the largest influencers are akin to media companies plugged into large segments of the population through its blogs and profiles and able to compete with newspapers, television and radio stations for the attention of users and ad-revenues.

Influencers are a growing market that can impact trends, politics and opinions by inspiring their followers to reflect as well as act. A representative survey from the Media Research and Innovation Center at the University of Southern Denmark disclosed that more than half of all Danish youth have been inspired by influencers to purchase a product, and more than one third have visited a place recommended by an influencer. Youth find inspiration in influencers when it comes to "picking clothes", "eating certain things," or having a "particular opinion" (Mehlsen 2020).

Sizable social media profiles known for other work e.g., music or sports, but still use their profiles for sponsorships, are less likely to be viewed as influencers by their followers (Mehlsen 2020). As a result, the uptake of their messages may be more effective compared to profiles which have sought fame through social platforms and commercial content only. Their followers are simply more unguarded.

One may also be famous for another vocation and at the same time function as an influencer trading social capital for monetary or political capital. One example is the American singer-songwriter Taylor Swift who regularly writes about her cats and otherwise flamboyant lifestyle on her social platform profiles, but is otherwise not much known for her political engagement. However, during the US midterm elections in 2018 she broke her silence and announced that she would be voting for the Democrats. In the same post she appealed to her 112+ million Instagram followers to register to vote, which led to a marked increase in voter registration: In less than 48 h, 169,000 people were newly registered—an upturn that vote.org attributed to a 'Taylor Swift effect'.[7] To mobilize this many new voters in a few days is more than the entire US federal government can do in 3 months. Two years later on October 7th 2020 Taylor Swift declared on her Instagram profile and in *V Magazine*, that she would vote for presidential candidate Joe Biden. Whether this incited a 'Taylor Swift-effect' remains unknown, but the mechanism is clear: Swift as an influencer trades social capital for political capital and democratic mobilization.

5.2 Superspreaders

With the emergence of the Covid-19 pandemic a new term, 'superspreaders', nudged its way into everyday language. A superspreader is a person who can pass a transmittable disease to multiple parties in a very short time. Large profiles on social platforms are another kind of superspreader who can 'infect' a lot of people, not with disease, but with (mis)information, packaged entertainment and opinions that spread like ripples on water.

Digital superspreaders have played a central role in the Covid-19 infodemic that emerged alongside the pandemic. One of the largest superspreaders of Covid-19 misinformation in 2020 wasn't an obscure conspiracy theorist or an army of Russian trolls, but the former US president, Donald J. Trump. This was the conclusion reached by a group of

---

[7] Gabbat, A. (2018). "The Taylor Swift effect: Nashville sounds off on singer's political endorsements", *The Guardian*, 12.10.2018, verified 08.01.2022: https://www.theguardian.com/music/2018/oct/12/taylor-swift-democrats-midterm-election-celebrity-political-endorsements

researchers from Cornell University after having analyzed 38 million English language articles on the pandemic from January to May 2020. In addition, Trump was mentioned in 37.7% of all media coverage on misinformation.[8] Trump shared misinformation on all public debate channels, as well as his own social media profiles, during press conferences and at public hearings.

Miracle cures were the most widespread misinformation theme during the period where Trump yielded an enormous bullhorn. In the spring of 2020, Trump touted the anti-malarial drug hydroxychloroquine as protection against Covid-19[9]; he also suggested that disinfectants such as bleach could be injected into the body to fight coronavirus. Trump's two eldest sons were central in spreading misinformation and conspiracy theories, e.g. that the pandemic was initiated to hurt Trump's impeachment case.

Similarly, a group of researchers from the Election Integrity Partnership concluded in their report, *The Long Fuse: Misinformation and the 2020 election,* that it was only a few large social media profiles which played decisive roles in framing the grand narrative of the stolen presidential election which led to the January sixth Capitol Hill siege in 2021. The scientists distilled the central narratives that surfaced on Facebook, Instagram, Twitter, YouTube and TikTok, in the months before and after the November 2020 presidential election. It was during this period that the narratives on election fraud and missing ballots began to spread and provoke unrest.[10]

[8] Evanega, S. et al. (2021). "Corona virus misinformation: quantifying sources and themes in the COVID-19 'infodemic'". Preprint, verified 28.06.2121: https://int.nyt.com/data/documenttools/evanega-et-al-coronavirus-misinformation-submitted-07-23-20-1/080839ac0c22bca8/full.pdf

[9] Niburski, K., & Niburski, O. (2020). "Impact of Trump's Promotion of Unproven COVID-19 Treatments and Subsequent Internet Trends: Observational Study," *Journal of medical Internet research*, *22*(11), e20044. https://doi.org/10.2196/20044

[10] Center for an Informed Public, Digital Forensic Research Lab, Graphika & Stanford Internet Observatory (2021). *The Long Fuse: Misinformation and the*

The report shows that influencers are embedded in, and utilize, a larger media ecosystem: Before and after the presidential election 2020, false election related posts were shared on social platforms by more or less random profiles with a small number of followers. Influencers and other large profiles elevated this 'grassroots content' to a larger more coherent narrative on election fraud and spread the narrative across platforms to an enormous audience. When the posts of influencers generated a sufficient amount of likes and engagement, established media paid notice and made stories of their own—and so it came full circle, when the narratives were promoted back onto social platforms.

Influencers are often considered trustworthy role models for their followers and may reach a large number of people almost instantaneously, that is, before a platform or fact-checker entity may assess the content of their messaging. And fact-checking isn't made easier when one of the largest superspreaders of misinformation is the president of an entire country. *The Long Fuse* report on *Misinformation and the 2020 election* shows examples of how a tweet from the former official Twitter profile @realDonaldTrump, an account then with more than 89 million followers at the time, initiated the spread of a false narrative on the platform. Trump tweeted that the electronic voting company responsible for the presidential election had either deleted Trump's votes or turned them into votes for Joe Biden. This led to 460.000 retweets and contributed greatly to building a conspiracy theory of electoral fraud.[11]

2020 Election. Stanford Digital Repository: Election Integrity Partnership. v1.3.0, verified 27.06.21: https://purl.stanford.edu/tr171zs0069

[11] Paul, K. (2021). "A few rightwing 'super-spreaders' fueled bulk of election falsehoods, study says", *The Guardian*, 05.03.2021, verified 15.08.2021:

https://www.theguardian.com/us-news/2021/mar/05/election-misinformation-trump-rightwing-super-spreader-study

When people with many followers on social platforms province roles as superspreaders, it doesn't only have to be on misinformation and other subprime content. According to the *Reuters Institute Digital News 2020* report, influencers and other celebrities played an important role on social platforms during the pandemic, by using the platforms to run online exercise classes and concerts, provide healthcare commentary and other initiatives that helped inform users or bring a collective online experience to life. *Reuters* points out that while social platforms may be used to spread misinformation they can just as well be used to spread trustworthy information and provide support in an era defined by anxiety and social distancing.[12]

The same trend was also seen elsewhere around the globe. In Denmark several celebrities and influencers began disseminating Covid-19 related content in 2020 with messages from the Danish Health Authorities on the importance of social distancing and masks, along with entertaining activities that provided followers with a sense of belonging through collective singing, dancing and quiz contests. Influencer channels were also used by politicians and authorities as a means to target certain groups in fighting Covid-19. On March 13, 2020, the Danish State Department held its first ever press conference in collaboration with an influencer. This happened when Danish Prime Minister, Mette Frederiksen, appeared on a Danish influencer, Alexander Husum's YouTube channel, which at the time had almost 400,000 followers, and asked youth to uphold social distancing recommendations.

On September 20th 2020 Mette Frederiksen also wrote "Hi, all followers of Anders" on another prominent Danish influencer, Anders Hemmingsen's, Instagram profile with more than one million followers. The Prime Minister went

---

[12] Newman, N. et al. (2020). *Reuters Institute Digital News Report 2020*, verified 15.08.2021: https://www.digitalnewsreport.org/survey/2020/

on to encourage concrete behavioral change: Youth should party less and use the covid infection tracking app. The Danish Prime Minister had also previously posted about Covid-19 on Anders Hemmingsen's and other influencer profiles (Fig. 5.1).

A representative survey from the Danish Media Research and Innovation Center report, *Influencers—the new young media outlets,* found that three out of four high school youth think that "it's ok that the government makes use of influencers to convey societally important events, like the coronavirus" (Mehlsen 2020).

The majority of youth use Facebook or Instagram for news, here influencers moreover play salient roles. Even though influencers aren't known for newscasting, they practically work as channels where youth consume news or comment on current events and cases in society (Mehlsen 2020). Influencers increasingly play a significant role in spreading information about socially relevant events and movements on social platforms, e.g., themes related to identity politics such as Black Lives Matter, #MeToo, cancel culture and Woke trends. Likewise, there is an increasing expectation that influencers make their voices heard when it comes to events that have great societal impact such as the Covid-19 pandemic. Influencers are part of a growing publicist circuit, where they exist in a realm between entertainment, opinion and journalism (Fig. 5.2) and compete for the attention of media users (Fig. 5.3).

Critical media coverage and public discourse on the subject of influencers typically cover two problematic issues: Critical coverage is directed at bad influencer marketing such as concealed, illegal or out-of-bounds advertisements directed at minors. Or else it criticizes harmful influencer content (e.g. influencers who go too far in terms of promoting harmful challenges, hate speech, misinformation, morally questionable traveling habits, disrespectful behavior).

andershemmingsendk ✔

•••

♡ ◯ ◁   ◻

584.916 views · Liked by **tilouhu**

andershemmingsendk Statsministeren har en vigtig besked · Lyt med her.

(@mette)

View all 723 comments

Fig. 5.2 **"Hi all followers of Anders**." Danish Prime Minister Mette Frederiksen has an important message about joining forces against the coronavirus on Anders Hemmingsen's Instagram channel, March 2020 (Andershemmingsen.dk on Instagram 18.03.2021, verified 15.08.2021: https://www.instagram.com/tv/B94DJOCHrWo/?utm_source=ig_embed)

Criticism of influencers rudimentary centers on whether they should be held accountable for their content and marketing; this is reflected in the political debate about whether the biggest influencers should be subject to press ethics rules and codes of conduct, as they reach a large swath of the

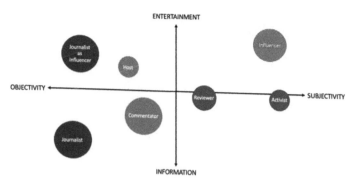

Fig. 5.3 Personal media is gaining traction in the attention economy, where media personalities navigate between information and entertainment; between striving for objectivity and subjectivity (Mehlsen 2020)

population and thereby accordingly grow to thus acquire editorial responsibility.[13]

One may easily overlook the growing role of influencers, whether it be good or bad, in everyday lives of users, established media, the political debate and the democratic conversation (Mehlsen 2020). Dismissed is furthermore the defining role that social platforms have when it comes to how influencers impact their followers.

Platforms seemingly operate as backstage editors when they moderate the content that influencers share. Social platforms are not only instrumental in spreading influencers' media content, they additionally have a final say on the content itself. For instance, you might unknowingly stumble upon a filter that removes a picture, a post or even your entire profile. Or the platform recommendation system might downgrade or mute your content, which means that your content won't be visible to very many users.

---

[13] Dr.dk (2019). "Minister: Stil bloggere til ansvar for indhold", Dr.dk 08.07.2019, verified 15.08.2021: https://www.dr.dk/nyheder/indland/minister-stil-bloggere-til-ansvar-indhold

Sustainability activist and influencer Gittemarie Johansen experienced the phenomenon as follows:

> It was a huge problem that there were a lot of influencers in Zero Waste-communities that were totally muted when they tried to talk about what was happening in Argentina. All the while people who talk about dietary products and cheap sweatshop clothing are allowed to spread their message unhindered (Mehlsen 2020).

Influencer Anders Hemmingsen chose to focus on one platform, Facebook's Instagram, making his business model extra vulnerable. Hemmingsen says, it feels like having a hidden employer (Mehlsen 2020):

> I've never heard from Facebook. I've never heard 'Hi, Anders, it's really cool what you're doing,' or 'Hey, it's absolutely not ok what you've done,' I haven't heard a thing." (...) One can say I haven't met my boss. I don't know who it is. I have no clue who I'm actually working under and who has the greatest power. And so it seems a little strange to work for someone you don't know. One creates content for their apps so they can go on making a living, in return they can delete an image without having to explain why, just as they can delete your profile without actually telling you why, except for referencing some standard procedure. So it's really strange. It's also a bit weird that you don't really know who's on the other end.

5.3   Feed the Algorithm, Eat or Be Eaten

Influencers are subject to the ruleset of platforms, such as permissible content and what best 'feeds the algorithm'. In the attention economy you can—also as an influencer— place your bets on proliferating content that attracts a lot of user attention. However, if you go too far, you may very well be muted.

Logan Paul was a rising YouTube star until he in December 2017 visited Japan's Aokigahara forest also known as the "Suicide Forest" and uploaded a video entitled "We found a dead body in the Japanese Suicide Forest" to his more than 15 million subscribers, mainly very young. The video raised uproar and turned into a huge scandal for Logan Paul; the sponsors left him and YouTube temporarily demonetized him. "YouTube demonetization" means that the content creator will not be able to receive money from a video or even from the entire channel.

YouTube has a "three strikes" policy meaning that if a creator repeatedly violates YouTube's rules, it may result in the creator's account being deleted. According to YouTube CEO Susan Wojcicki, Logan Paul should not be banned from the platform despite the controversy in the aftermath of his video. At a media conference in California in February 2018, Wojcicki said about Logan Paul:

> He hasn't done anything that would cause those three strikes (…) We can't just be pulling people off our platform (…) They need to violate a policy. We need to have consistent [rules]. This is like a code of law.[14]

In 2021, Logan Paul, and his new boxing videos and podcast *Impaulsive*, has made a major comeback on YouTube being featured as number 9 on *Forbes Magazine's* ranking of the highest-paid YouTubers.

Attention is a fleeting construct that may be moved and directed toward more clicks, likes and engagement—but

---

[14]Newton, C. (2018). "YouTube's CEO says Logan Paul doesn't deserve to be kicked off the platform", *The Verge*, 12.2.2018, verified 28.1.2022: https://www.theverge.com/2018/2/12/17006074/youtube-ceo-logan-paul-susan-wojcicki

may likewise be redirected, so that those who at one point commanded it, no longer receive the same level of attention. For this purpose, platform content moderation as well as deplatforming are effective tools. Deplatforming is the removal of one's account on social platforms for breaking platform rules (Rogers 2020). Where the algorithms of the leading platforms previously favored extreme profiles and content that propelled them into becoming influencers and 'Internet personalities'—a shift took place in the late 2010's where several extreme profiles were either suspended or 'deplatformed'. Milo Yiannopoulos and Alex Jones represent two far right profiles who became Internet celebrities sharing controversial content in the 2010's but were banned from leading social platforms in the late 2010's for being "dangerous individuals" (Rogers 2020).

Being deplatformed by Facebook, Instagram, Twitter, YouTube and other leading platforms has significant consequences for an influencer's visibility, maintenance of a fan base as well as revenue stream, and migrating to alternative social platforms may not add much (Rogers 2020).

When a leading social platform, such as YouTube or Facebook, chooses to shut down a profile, it also has significant repercussions for the public presence of that person. Former President Donald J. Trump got to experience this first hand when his channels were banned from various platforms in January 2021 and he instead attempted to start his own blog. The blog, *From the Desk of Donald J. Trump*, went live in May 2021 but closed after just 29 days and after only 2000 users had shared content from it to other social platforms. In comparison to Trump's viral heyday, when he boasted 88 million followers on Twitter and had a staggering number of shares, these numbers were a drop in the ocean for one of the leading superspreaders of the infodemic.[15] Marching to your own drums once banned from other marching bands also explains Donald J. Trump's initiative to start his own social network and app with the telling title Truth Social projected to launch in the Spring of 2022. Interesting side note according to *The Verge's* reporting: "Truth Social describes each individual post as a "truth" in the app's description. The retweet equivalent is apparently called a "re-truth"", so "truth" may aggregate, multiply but not divide inside the true social eco-system.[16]

Even though social platforms are tightening their grip on profiles that they deem 'dangerous', i.e., profiles that incite unrest or threaten public health, there is no sign that the phenomenon of influencers and other large profiles is becoming an endangered species. On the contrary, the biggest profiles are receiving more online attention and gaining more and more followers on platforms, with a steadily increasing number of users.

5.4 Ad-dicted

The products the influencer promote—from Nike sneakers to views on fiscal policy, #Metoo and Black Lives Matter, are as recognizable as they are vetted by the identity profile of the influencer in question. For the user they appear as personalized messages and ads—more or less hidden—but in any event personalized to "me" as user who has voluntarily decided to follow the influencer. Every follower may

---

[15] Harwell, D. & Dawsey, J. (2021). "Trump ends blog after 29 days, infuriated by measly readership", *The Washington Post*, 02.06.2021, verified 15.08.2021: https://www.washingtonpost.com/technology/2021/06/02/trump-blog-dead/

[16] Peters, J. (2022). "Trump's Truth Social app will apparently launch in February", *The Verge*, 06.01.2022, verified 08.01.2022: https://www.theverge.com/2022/1/6/22871167/trump-truth-social-app-network-launch-february-tmtg

accordingly gain personal ownership of the ads with which one is confronted in the public space given by the influencer's profile, again provided by the social platform of choice. To claim ownership to personalized ads is a way to making the users addicted. An addict is first in sooth an addict by the time identified ownership of the addiction is realized.

All agents in the attention economic ecosystem, whether influencers, platforms, advertisers, media or users, are addicted to and dictated by ads. Addicted to ads as the base for the entire business model making in turn action on the social platforms appear free, smooth, efficient, voluntary, beneficial, profitable and personalized. The actors are at the same time dictated by ads. If the ads don't work in the attention economy the influencers are not going to promote them; advertisers and sponsors do not care to pay, the media will not allocate air time and newspaper columns while users are not going to spend their scarce time on what doesn't work and nobody apparently cares about.

Attention is something you buy your way to in terms of social capital or hard cash, and the receiving end pays with attention (and data), so ads control and dictate what happens in the entire ecosystem. All involved parties are *ad-dicted*.

6

Clandestine Casino

"In the casino, the cardinal rule is to keep them playing and to keep them coming back. The longer they play, the more they lose, and in the end, we get it all."

— Robert De Niro, *Casino*

No Limit Texas Hold 'em, Roulette, Blackjack, Baccarat and not least slot machines are mostly associated with Caesars Palace or MGM Grand in Las Vegas, Casino Barrière d'Enghien-les-Bains in France or Casino de Monte Carlo in Monaco. It may seem there is no immediate connection between these and platforms such as Facebook, Twitter, Instagram, Snapchat, TikTok, YouTube, Twitch, LinkedIn, Messenger, WhatsApp or WeChat. But Casinos, online games and social platforms have one thing in common: Their application of well-known psychological mechanisms and hidden tricks of the trade to capture and retain peoples' attention at the green table, slot-machine or screen in order to gain, win and control.

The like button, retweets and red notifications are examples of user-experience design not only tapping into the depths of users' need for feedback, cohesion and recognition,

© The Author(s), under exclusive license to Springer Nature Switzerland AG 2022
V. F. Hendricks, C. Mehlsen, *The Ministry of Truth*,
https://doi.org/10.1007/978-3-030-98629-2_6

but also having a mountainous impact on user behavior. The casino industry has long since figured out how to create an illusion of free will and self-determination; social platforms and online gaming are taking this illusion to whole new heights by virtually creating a clandestine casino.

6.1   Weapons of Mass Distraction

Players or users are under the illusion that they voluntarily do as they please and of their own volition. The interesting question to ask is *why* gamblers at the casino or users of social platforms behave the way they do? An important answer to this question may be found in the so-called Skinner box.

In the 1930s, Harvard psychologist B.F. Skinner made a series of behavioral discoveries in the course of his conducted rat experiments that have since found their way into casinos, online games and social platforms. Skinner placed a hungry rat in a box with a release device or lever on one side. When the hungry rat roamed the box to find food, it would occasionally bump into the release device and trigger a treat. After being placed in the box a few times the rat had learned to trigger the release, without delay, to get its treat. Skinner went on to assert that this reward enhanced behavior applied to any 'operant' whether rat or human. Human behavior may be swayed sometimes even controlled like in the Skinner box. When people return to a casino or get stuck in a feed, it's because they expect some kind of reward, a like, an upvote, a comment, a share or some other kind of response from other users.

The expectation of a potential reward may become ever more intense when not knowing when it will be granted. It makes one stick around for a little bit longer and return more often. Skinner discovered this mechanism after conducting additional experiments. These experiments, which would go on to be at least as important as his first, established that if the rat received the same reward every time the lever was pulled, it would only trigger the device when hungry. If the aim is to get the rodent to maximize the number device releases, then its rewards need to vary. If the rat doesn't know whether it will get rewarded a treat, or extras or none at all, when it triggers the device, it will trigger the device again and again. The rat has become 'hooked' or addicted. The rodent doesn't know if it will get its treat when it triggers the release device just as the gambler doesn't know if he or she will win the next round on the slot-machine, and so they keep pulling the lever in the Skinner box or slot machine.

In behavioral psychology, the above is referred to as the *principle of variable reward*—the sub-branch of psychology studying the nuts and bolts of variable rewards is sometimes even referred to as random rewards psychology. While a human is not literally a rat or rodent, there are similarities as to how rats and humans react to this principle. As with the Skinner box, the principle of variable or random reward also applies to social platforms: Rewards are triggered at different and unpredictable times. When users go to open their Instagram, Snapchat or Tinder profiles they do not know if anyone has *liked* their picture, left a comment, made a 'lol' status update, or even left a personal message. Like gamblers at a casino, reward uncertainty guarantees social platforms that its users will stick around—a weapon of mass distraction where the house always wins.

Rewards like upvotes, likes, posted comments or shares are positive feedbacks that triggers dopamine (Klanker et al. 2015). Dopamine is a neurotransmitter in the brain that make us feel short bursts of pleasure. And so, when we feel compelled to check our SoMe profile and there is a reward waiting, our brain gets a boost of dopamine. As users we are unable to short-circuit this boost—for instance, some posts will receive a lot of likes, others very few or none at all, which in turn works to keep the positive feedback *unpredictable*.

Many users feel compelled to frequently log in, to see if there's a reward (Eyal 2014). Secondly, the unpredictability of the reward leads to increased production of dopamine, contributing to increased platform engagement. This engagement may be refined with various reactions, such as a world of emojis and emoticons that add to the unpredictability of the feedback structure and its reward dynamics.

Social platforms naturally want to generate more traffic, and therefore make a germane effort to stimulate reaction triggers that contribute to the innate human desire for recognition and cohesion. Since the positive feedback of others is not guaranteed by posting Wednesday to Thursday or by sharing Tuesday to Saturday, users will actively seek to get ever more feedback by posting and sharing Monday, Friday and Sunday. And so users engage (by posting, commenting and 'liking') on the platform's gameboard where they 'gamble' hoping to receive positive feedback or social reward. The underlying business model of social platforms uses psychological mechanisms similar to Skinner boxes by exploiting the basic human need to feel connected, approved and recognized by other users and to receive feedback and rewards accordingly.

By the end of the twentieth century, Skinnner's rat experiments were virtually forgotten. However, they were thoroughly dusted off by the American professor B.J. Fogg when he came up with the idea that computers can influence human behaviour if they contain triggers similar to the Skinner box device. Fogg took behavioral psychology to the next level and created a new interdisciplinary field that he dubbed 'behavioral design' and then applied its mindset to develop new digital services.

Had Fogg been at a university in Copenhagen, Cologne or Cambridge, the discipline might not have seeped into the heart of Silicon Valley. But Fogg was a professor at Stanford University, south of San Francisco—practically next door to the budding BigTech companies, and so behavioral design became central Silicon Valley operations. For example, Yahoo, Google and Hewlett-Packard were founded by Stanford University alumni. Around the millennium Fogg's classes in behavioral design and his seminal textbook in the field *Persuasive Technology: Using Computers to Change What we Think and Do* (2002) hatched a number of tech-entrepreneurs such as Mike Krieger who founded Instagram. Prior Facebook stockholder Robert McNamee writes in his book *Zucked: Waking up to the Facebook Catastrophe* (2019), that apps created by Foggs' students were especially apt at capturing user attention:

> His insight was that computing devices allow programmers to combine psychology and persuasion concepts from early twentieth century, like propaganda, with techniques from slot machines, like variable rewards, and tie them to the human social need for approval and validation in ways that few users can resist. (McNamee 2019)

Fogg's model for behavioral design rests on the notion that behavior may be altered when:

1. A person is motivated.
2. A person is able to perform the action.
3. A trigger helps to set off the action.

A digital trigger may be a notification that pops up on your cell phone to say 'hi, look here and click here' and voila, you're all of a sudden motivated and open the app (the action). Social platforms and online game developers know very well what motivate and trigger us as humans. Facebook,

Instagram and WhatsApp notifications are not randomly the color red, just as unread mail in your inbox probably are. Red is a warning signal that calls for attention and an emotional as well as tangible response.[1]

Other people's feedback is indeed what triggers us, as the brain releases pleasant, addictive chemical compounds in response to social interactions. This is why we constantly nudge each other for feedback. The dots in text messages, also called "typing awareness indicator," actually work as means for nudging each other: If you receive a message on Messenger or in iMessages from a friend and begin answering it, your friend can see three dots in the message field as an indication that you're typing a reply (Fig. 6.1). Your friend then stays a little longer … what's behind the dots?

6.2   Time in the Zone

Casinos, online games and social platforms all use behavioral design to keep gamers/users engaged. They have this in common because their business models are based on the same principle: The more time we spend on the machine or app, the better it is for business. This is why machines are designed to maximize 'time on device' i.e., time spent on the cell phones, tablets and consoles. Casinos' call it gambler *retention* or play-and-stay, while social platforms call it user *engagement* but it all winds up in same pecuniary place. Time spent on the playground of social platforms ends up as money in the providers pocket through user-profiling, data-harvesting and advertisement sales.

---

[1] Herman, J. (2018). "How Tiny Red Dots Took you're your Life", *New York Times*, 27.02.2018, verified 19.06.2021: https://www.nytimes.com/2018/02/27/magazine/red-dots-badge-phones-notification.html

Fig. 6.1 "Someone's typing..." – the typing awareness indicator

A casino needs to accommodate a lot of different people, and not all gamblers are the same—from high-rollers and compulsive whales to habitual fish and small potatoes. Casinos monitor, collect behavioral data and profile their different guests in ways that are reminiscent of how social platforms profile users to create efficient and individualized user experiences. Because casinos cater to everyone from exclusive high-rollers for the expensive poker and Blackjack tables, to hotel guests that just need to go to the restaurant or hotel elevator, or to random walk-ins that might be interested in everything from Baccarat and slot-machines to roulette, it needs to have the appearance of a showcase for entertainment and potential winnings baked into its design and décor. Not a Ring that can rule them all as in the *Lord of the Rings*, but a casino that can rule them all (Fig. 6.2).[2]

The American cultural anthropologist Natasha Schüll conducted several anthropological studies of casinos in Las Vegas focused on décor and architecture and authored *Addiction by Design: Machine Gambling in Las Vegas* (2012). While reading a design manual, Natascha Schüll learned that

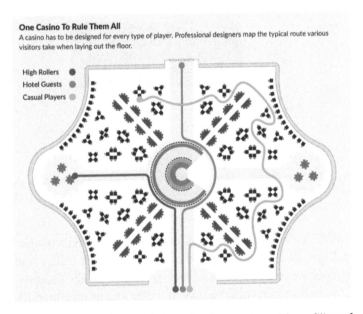

One Casino To Rule Them All
A casino has to be designed for every type of player. Professional designers map the typical route various visitors take when laying out the floor.

High Rollers
Hotel Guests
Casual Players

Fig. 6.2 A typical interior design plan for a casino with profiling of guests (Null, C. (2015). "An Inside Look: The Secrets of Casino Design", 888 Casino, verified 23.01.2021: https://www.888casino.com/blog/the-secrets-behind-casino-design)

[2] Null, C. (2015). "An Inside Look: The Secrets of Casino Design", *888 Casino*, verified 23.01.2021: https://www.888casino.com/blog/the-secrets-behind-casino-design

the stated purpose of casino design is to make the gambler "not analyze the various things you observe as you meander along, we want to curve you to where we want you."[3] Concretely, this means that casinos avoid sharp angles e.g., in carpeting, as a 90° angle signals an abrupt break.

The casino industry has experimented with interior planning throughout time, though mostly with the overarching architectural concept of one entrance and one exit or that all routes lead to the opulent casino with all the wealth that can flow to the lucky winner (Fig. 6.2). When people first enter, they need to be retained physically. Either through a labyrinthine layout that confuses them so much that it's difficult to find the exit. Or as the industry has embarked on lately: to find inspiration in open and inviting playgrounds with round corners, soft arches, friendly angles and an assortment of activities, one cannot help but try. In this sense the casino is more akin to a theme park or recreational spa; comfortable, fun and relaxing and where you don't mind spending money on what is perceived as an option, but which in the final analysis is designed to end up in the pocket of the casino. One doesn't have to worry about time either, as there's no such thing as meeting "by the clock" as at the railway station, since clocks are notoriously absent from the casino decor.[4]

Nothing is left to chance at a casino, especially not the placement of its slot-machines—this is where the big money is made. In the 1970s, slot machines made up almost 40% of casino profits in Las Vegas. Today it's almost 70%. The recent success of slot-machines can, in large part, be attributed to touchscreens. Touchscreens give designers a wealth of

[3] Center for Humane Technology (2012). *Your Undivided Attention* podcast, episode 1, verified 06.23.2021: https://www.humanetech.com/podcast

[4] Mullennix, B. (2020). "Why Casinos Don't Have Clocks or Windows (Explained!), *Feeling Vegas*, 21.09.2020, verified 8.07.2021: https://www.feelingvegas.com/why-casinos-dont-have-clocks-windows/

opportunity to create many different and interchangeable designs that reflect pop culture and the zeitgeist of the moment. According to Shüll, digitization is the reason for slot-machines winning territory. Digitization provides casinos with greater control over the odds, which means players may be tempted with higher returns and more exciting games, while simultaneously ensuring the casino the biggest slice of the pie.[5]

Casinos are designed so gamblers end up in the 'zone'. The zone is the state where one continually keeps pulling the slot machine, plays endless rounds of Blackjack and suspends all real-life everyday worries. Natasha Schüll describes the zone as an affective state where one feels sheltered and decoupled from time, place and body. While Shüll conducted her anthropological studies of casinos she repeatedly heard gamblers, compulsive gamblers in particular, use the term 'zone'. For the compulsive gambler, the zone is the most desirable state of ludomania. It is a persistent state of normalcy and carefreeness that diminishes a player's worries and pain while gambling. Shüll met a woman who suffered from narcolepsy and uncontrollable sleeping bouts. The woman told her that she could fall asleep while driving on the highway and while having sex. The only place she couldn't sleep was while she played video poker.[6]

The zone is indeed a state that can be enriching and creative, but also highly addictive. If you get stuck in the feed you can end up in the zone where one imperceptibly loses one's sense of time and place, watching ever more videos chosen by a personalized user experience-tapping algorithm. As

[5] Plumer, B. (2015). "Slot-machine science", Vox.com 01.03.2015, verified 08.08.2021: https://www.vox.com/2014/8/7/5976927/slot-machines-casinos-addiction-by-design

[6] Center for Humane Technology: *Your Undivided Attention* podcast, episode 1, verified 23.06.2021: https://www.humanetech.com/podcast

an 18 year old remarked on being suspended in a platform feed: "The other day I spent 11 h on TikTok in a single day" (Mehlsen 2020). It's no coincidence that new content emerges at the top of the feed every time you drag a finger down the screen on Instagram, TikTok and many other social platforms.

The longer gamblers or users linger in the casino or on a social platform, the more behavioral and consumer pattern data is harvested; this leads to stronger predictability of what gamblers or users might think and do in the future which, in turn, facilitates an even more expansive and customized personalization of the user experience. The greater the power of predictability, the tighter the grip casinos and BigTech have on gamblers and users, which paves the way for more opportunities of manipulation. The connection to the casino goes full circle when tech platforms not only control the news, friend and follower requests, and the maintenance of one's social network, but also offer data harvesting online games.

6.3   The Boom of Online Gaming

Data-harvesting is a crucial element in the development of online games. Online gaming is the most lucrative entertainment industry in the world, and digital behavioral design is a means of capturing and keeping players online. The annual turnover of the gaming industry is expected to reach $200 billion by 2023, while the music industry, in comparison, was valued at $20 billion dollars in 2020.[7]

---

[7] Wijman, T. (2021). "Global Games Market to Generate $175.8 Billion in 2021; Despite a Slight Decline, the Market Is on Track to Surpass $200 Billion in 2023", *Newzoo*, 06.05.2021, verified 23.6.2021:

https://newzoo.com/insights/articles/global-games-market-to-generate-175-8-billion-in-2021-despite-a-slight-decline-the-market-is-on-track-to-surpass-200-billion-in-2023/

The largest growth is in mobile gaming which grew significantly during the Covid-19 pandemic. Globally, of the more than 2.7 billion who played online in 2020, 2.6 billion did so on mobile devices. The majority of online games are free to download, and only a little more than a third pay to play on their cell phone.[8]

The business model is called Free2Play (F2P) or freemium—so how do game developers make money? One source of income is microtransactions, where gamers spend money buying in-app game items such as special weapons or virtual currency. *Fortnite,* the freemium game from Epic Games generates the vast majority of its income from microtransactions and from the game currency V-Bucks in particular. However, the gaming industry's business model is increasingly dependent on advertisement technology (adtech) which collects and analyses gamer data and uses advertisement as an independent source of income and as a strategy to attract new users. But as the saying goes, there is no such thing as a free lunch: While gaming for free on mobile devices, players become the product, while advertisers, in fact, are the real customers—exactly the same as for social platforms.

Just like social platforms, the gaming industry data-harvest to psychologically profile players so it becomes facile to micro-target commercial content. When players interact with one another and move around in the game environment they create data points for the game platform's algorithm. This may be data on weapon preferences, how they are used and on what kinds of conversations players have with others

---

[8] Reuters (2021). "Report: Gaming revenue to top $159B in 2020", *Reuters*, 12.05.2020, verified 23.06.2021: https://www.reuters.com/article/esports-business-gaming-revenues-idUSFLM8jkJMl

during gameplay.[9] There is nothing new about dividing game player's psychological profiles into categories such as 'achiever', 'explorer', 'socializer', 'killer' or some combination of these (Bartle 1996). What is new, is that the data may be used to predict behavior and influence gamer categories. Behavioral data not only says a lot about what motivates a gamer but also how they feel at any given time. If you are depressed, or on a diet, it will influence your gaming behavior.

Psychological profiling via data-harvest is part and parcel of the gaming industry. Political economist and game researcher, David Nieburg, was surprised by the furor of the public debate once it became known that Cambridge Analytica, a political consultancy company, had harvested the data of millions of Facebook users and used these data to micro-target political advertisements through psychological profiling:

> Why are people so upset? The gaming industry has been doing this for a long time, only for a different goal: just to make a lot of money. Nobody gets too upset about games. But the underlying technology is really powerful.[10]

A pressing issue with harvesting online gaming data is that minors make up a large segment of the gamer population. The age limit for playing online games and creating profiles on social platforms such as TikTok, Instagram and Snapchat in many countries is 13 years of age. However, it is extremely easy for children to bypass age restrictions, even though the platform is obliged to attain parental consent or some other

---

[9] IDA (2021). "Onlinespil gambler med børns data", published by IDA & Dataethics. Copenhagen.

[10] Tiffany, K. (2019). "Angry Birds and the end of privacy", *Vox*, 14.05.2021, verified 25.06.2021: https://www.vox.com/explainers/2019/5/7/18273355/angry-birds-phone-games-data-collection-candy-crush

form of age verification to ensure that its data collection and processing are legal.

The British 5Rights Foundation report, "Disrupted Childhood—The Cost of Persuasive Design", from 2018, highlights how digital services, such as online games, systematically implement manipulative behavioral designs into their products aiming at collecting personal data for commercial use.[11] Children are particularly vulnerable and easy to affect through behavioral design. For instance, the report "Online Games Gamble with Child Safety" published by the Danish Engineers' Association IDA and the DataEthics think tank mention a long list of games that use emotionally manipulative techniques to get users to watch commercials and/or spend money in a game. The freemium game, *Doctor Kids*, developed by Slovenian company Bubadu, contains commercials and in-app purchasing offers: *Doctor Kids* made its game characters cry if children didn't make an in-game purchase.

Free online games for small children make up a large part of App Store and Google Play and are often marketed as 'educational' i.e., for informational and learning purposes. A lot of the games encourage children to share their progress on social platforms, sometimes in exchange for a reward such as coins or a game item. For example, in *Candy Crush Saga*, players are encouraged to connect the game to their Facebook profiles so they can share their progress with friends.

Digital behavioral design may tempt and even force players to watch commercials. While researching the report "Online Games Gamble with Child Safety" (IDA 2021) Danish journalist Mie Oehlenschläger and a 12-year-old boy tried to see what would happen if he downloaded and played

---

[11] Kidron, D. et al. (2018). *Disrupted Childhood. The Cost of Persuasive Design*, 5Rights Foundation, verified 06.23.21: https://5rightsfoundation.com/static/5Rights-Disrupted-Childhood.pdf

Subway Surfers on an iPhone 6 for 30 min.[12] *Subway Surfers*, a hugely successful Danish game and one of the most downloaded games in the world between 2010 and 2020, rewards its users for watching commercials. Within half an hour the boy found that by watching the commercials, he would receive items, such as keys, that helped him survive in the game. By watching commercials he was able to survive in overtime instead of getting squashed; he could also double the value of 'loot boxes' and receive extra coins that he could then use to purchase in-game items. Several commercials lasted up to 20 s and the boy had to watch them to the very end in order to continue playing. The boy experienced being trapped 'inside' a commercial by an emoji-game, that he had to play in order to resume his original game. He was shown Nerf toy weapons, the board game Clue and instant noodle commercials. In the shop, he was asked to use real money to purchase skins and other game items.

Gaming is not merely about playing the game, it is also about watching others play and participating in game groups. Gaming is therefore both an interactive activity, a streaming activity and a social activity. In fact, watching gaming videos is an increasingly popular activity, with YouTube (Google/Alphabet owned) and Twitch (Amazon owned) being among the largest platforms for this sort of occupation. Facebook caught on and created a dedicated Facebook Gaming section where users can play games, watch gaming videos and participate in game groups. Measured by 'time on device' Facebook Gaming and Twitch grew enormously with the emergence of the Covid-19 pandemic. The numbers are staggering. For instance, in February 2021 alone, users spent a

---

[12] IDA (2021). "Onlinespil gambler med børns data", published by IDA and Dataethics, Copenhagen.

whopping 1.8 billion hours on Twitch and 400 million hours on Facebook Gaming.[13]

When online games and social platforms are capable of predicting with greater and greater certainty what users are thinking, it starts to resemble an increasingly precise information-based blueprint of human needs, desires, values and preferences. These can in turn be pushed and shoved in different directions depending on what one is interested in imposing on users; from café latte with oat milk, to vacation rentals, new skins and political views. What happens then to independent decision-making and free will?

6.4   Bounded Rationality and Two Systems

If humans were fully rational beings, then the strength of our free will would be proportional to how well informed we were, and we probably wouldn't fall for the glimmer of gimmicks and poor decisions. However, this isn't so, neither in theory nor in practice. Whether we like it or not, our rationality is bounded, which can be both advantageous and a source of exploitation.

The concept of bounded rationality was first coined by psychology professor and Nobel prize winner Herbert Simon in 1957, who also laid the bricks for attention economy (Chap. 2). Bounded rationality is Simon's response to his dissatisfaction with *homo economicus* model of man, the perfect rational agent of neoclassical economists, complete with unlimited attention, perfect information, unimpeded

---

[13] Stephen, B. (2021). "Twitch and Facebook Gaming exploded during the pandemic – and they're even bigger a year later", *The Verge*, 15.03.2021, verified 25.06.2021: https://www.theverge.com/2021/3/15/22331623/twitch-facebook-gaming-pandemic-hours-watched

computing powers, flawless memory and other ideal cognitive qualities.

This doesn't fit the bill of ordinary people and Simon therefore went on to launch an understanding of rationality that takes people's actual cognitive limitations into account:

> Broadly stated, the task is to replace the global rationality of economic man with the kind of rational behavior that is compatible with the access to information and the computational capacities that are actually possessed by organisms, including man, in the kinds of environments in which such organisms exist. (Simon 1955): 99

If a person were a full-blown *homo economicus*, he or she wouldn't miscalculate, make bad decisions, fall victim to financial bubbles and fall prey of deception or seduction. As it turns out people experience all of the above on a regular basis. This is why plenty of influential, descriptive as well as normative, theories in psychology, philosophy, computer science, cognitive science and behavioral studies that reject the notion of a perfect and unimpeded rationality, have made reference to Simon's concept of bounded rationality since its inception.

Man's bounded rationality is the foundation of psychology professor Daniel Kahneman's now legendary studies on human decision making and its processes. Kahneman unpacks these mechanisms in his 2011 bestseller *Thinking Fast and Slow*. A book that may be viewed as a reader-friendly mainstream testament to Kahneman's impressive contribution to the theoretical understanding of decision making and the psychology of choice. Kahneman's studies were initiated in the 1970s in collaboration with cognitive researcher and mathematician Amos Tversky (1937–1996); the two came to develop what they dubbed *prospect theory*, for which they were awarded the Nobel prize in economics in 2002.

Prospect theory is a behavioral model that demonstrates how humans choose between different alternatives that involve risk as well as uncertainty. An important point is that we as humans are *risk averse*, meaning that we avoid exposing ourselves to risks if possible: We care more about what we may gain, than what we equally might lose. Conversely, if there is a high probability for a smaller gain, then rather win little with certainty by being risk averse, than be a *risk seeker* with higher but less probable gains.

So, if there is a high probability of receiving a lot of likes on your next post, because your opinions align perfectly with your circle of friends, you will ultimately only fear being terribly disappointed and as a consequence avoid drawing your opinions more sharply—in this situation you've become *risk averse*. Conversely, if you assess that there is a high probability that your circle of friends does not like your opinion of, say the current president, but you nonetheless feel obliged to vent your opinion, you can merely hope for no further loss of standing when you take the chance and post it as is—in this scenario you're more *risk seeking*.

If your tell-all video of a celebrity is of such poor quality that one hardly can tell what is going on, but is still good enough to potentially harvest a lot of likes (if lucky), then you might as well send it into circulation without seeking permission to do so from the one you're about to expose. This is a prime example of risk seeking behavior. And finally: You become risk averse, if the current version of the TikTok video you're contemplating uploading has a slim chance of failing and is able to generate a lot of likes without having to add extra steps and a 'cheeky move' in fear of losing big (Table 6.1).

Prospect theory is applied in a wide variety of economic matters from consumer choice to labor market demand to the insurance industry (Barberis 2013) and is a central component of Kahneman's *Thinking Fast and Slow*. If one first

Table 6.1 Reward, loss and willingness to take risks (Kahneman and Tversky 1979; Kahneman 2011)

	Win	Lose
High probability	95% chance of winning $10.000	95% chance of losing $10.000
Certainty effect	Fear of disappointment	Hope to avoid loss
	RISK AVERSION	**RISK SEEKING**
Low probability	5% chance of winning $10.000	5% chance of losing $10.000
Possibility effect	Hope of big reward	Fear of big loss
	RISK SEEKING	**RISK AVERSION**

grasps how the bounded rationality of man is embedded in our decision making, in light of risk seeking and risk averse tendencies, then one is well on the way to attaining a more detailed understanding of the psychology of decision and human behavior. This knowledge may be applied to and exploited in casinos, on social platforms or in 'free' online games.

Kahneman divides the mental decision making capacities of humans into two systems, called *system one* and *system two*. Where system one largely works automatically and is fast and without much effort or a sense of voluntary control, system two allocates attention to the kind of mental activities that indeed crave and demand cognitive effort, such as complex calculations and reasoning out entangled leads. System two provides people with an innate subjective experience of self-agency and -determination, deliberate choice and thorough concentration (Kahneman 2011). While system one is concerned with intuitive decision making processes, typically derived from emotions, impulses, and immediate reactions to miscellaneous experiences or events, a person in system two approaches actions, events and situations thoughtfully and slowly with an intentional mental drive that directly mobilizes a conscious goal of exercising self-control.

All system two processes demand focused attention. But because attention is always directed towards something in particular, it may easily be derailed, as seen in Chap. 2, when the surrounding volume of information is an abundance and readily available. Because attention is always directed, we humans tend to multitask rather poorly, as when driving while scrolling through our cell phone or digital dashboard—until it is all out of (self-)control.

The interconnection of the two systems lies in the fast and intuitive system one, offering up decision scenarios and suggestions that system two then slowly and thoroughly evaluates, potentially leading to action. System two takes over when system one is on the brink of making a mistake in complex decision making scenarios or when in doubt. But because system two is slow, meticulous and "lazy" the individual will follow the law of least resistance in an attempt to spend as little mental energy as possible in making a decision. This is why the intuitive reactions of system one dominate everyday decision making. On the other hand it isn't because system one is without recall to past experience or merely approaches decision making from hand to mouth. As humans we are equipped with a considerable amount of *associative memory* through which we react automatically and with quick responses when exposed to certain stimuli. These stimuli recall thoughts and feelings from memory that are connected to stimuli we were previously exposed to. We are primed to certain deliberative, decisive and behavior patterns embedded in our associative memory, that are aligned with the *modus operandi* of system one.

This is merely reinforced by what Kahneman dubs the *exposure effect*. The exposure effect states that the more we as individuals are exposed to certain stimuli, such as likes, clicks, upvotes, comments, notifications, memes, videos, tweets or certain images, the more familiar and comfortable we become with these stimuli. And the greater the probability that we will develop a predilection for them. It is just as easy and familiar as an effortless cell phone maneuver that evokes positive feelings of well-being. The more we visit a social platform, the more we're exposed to its reward structure, and the more unpredictable feedback we harvest, the greater the probability that we will be subject to its underlying exposure effect. And so, we return again and again and again.

Here positive feelings are interpreted in such a way that the activity can be easily, safely and soundly delegated to the institution and continue unimpeded. For a person who goes down this route, it can mean becoming less critical, making fewer informed decisions and more often missing the mark of what is deemed socially acceptable behavior. *Affect heuristics* as defined by Kahneman, is the tendency of people to make decisions and have opinions based on the immediately available emotions that diminish uncertainty, negative experiences and too much effort. This emotional predisposition is the backdrop from which people come to evaluate their decisions as risky and uncertain, rather than beneficial and certain. The most important role of system one in decision making matters is thereby to secure an individual's understanding of what normalcy amounts to by continually (re) defining and calibrating the current decision making model and its accompanying associations and expectations of the future.

Because social platforms prime their users to seek positive feedback via an unpredictable reward structure, the users are more likely to expose themselves to the possibility effect. The prospect of large returns in terms of likes, comments or shares stimulates the willingness of users to seek risks, especially when the only alternative—a lower probability of going viral—lies with a handful of upvotes at best or even zero positive feedback. Here, a system one decision enters the equation, to run the risk of repeatedly spending an increasing amount of attention, while receiving no or negative social feedback, in hope of hitting the jackpot sooner or later with a post, image or share—a hope that by far outweighs the absence of feedback we experience on the way to jackpot.

If framed in terms of loss or gain, a majority will prefer to avoid negative social feedback rather than receive positive social feedback, that is, if it comes down to making a choice—negative feedback *feels* about twice as bad than the duplicate amount of positive feedback. Fear of a misstep, for example in an online debate, and receiving the 'hate' of others may help explain why so many young people avoid participating in Facebook debates.[14]

The experience of loss or gain is strengthened by the so-called *endowment effect*. It suggests that the more ownership we delegate to a particular person, a tense political issue, Covid-19 restrictions, a social platform or any other effect for that matter, the greater the emotional value we attach to both it and to our emotional response when experiencing loss.

System one and two along with associative memory, exposure-, possibility- and endowment effects, and risk behavior, in decision making matters are all core elements in the psychology of decisions. In many cases decisions are automatic, subconscious reflections and reactions for which individuals have no palpable control.

Others, however, may be interested in acquiring and exercising this kind of control. Casinos as well as online game

---

[14] Institut for Menneskerettigheder (2017). "Hadefylde ytringer i den offentlige online debat"; DUF (2016). "Unge fravælger debat. Tonen er for hård", 07.01.2016. Copenhagen.

services and social platforms operate under the guise that we the users merely do what we want.

Eventually the user will come to understand that a platform will reward certain social behaviors. If a specific social behavior has proved itself to be more or less consequential in accommodating certain psychological needs, it will, according to Kahneman's theory, embed itself into memory as a familiar and comforting experience that it is difficult to do without.

From the exposure effect it follows that the more a user is exposed to the stimuli of the platform, the easier it becomes to succumb to habit. We therefore subconsciously tend to repeat the same actions again and again, regardless of whether it's visiting a casino, a social platform or a game portal, in search of positive feedback through an ever evolving self-refining cycle.

6.5 Big Brother Between Pain and Pleasure

An almost century old science fiction novel captures how a regime can use distractions and exploit our hunger for dopamine as a means of regulating behavior. In the British author Aldous Huxley's disturbing science fiction dystopia, *Brave New World*, from 1932, Western citizens are cast into a strict social hierarchy, brainwashed to love their own oppression and forced into a medically induced happiness that comes in the form of the regime issued drug *soma*. The World State, endowed with the crazy vision of an ideal society, is ruled by 10 people only. One of them being Western leader Mustapha Mond. Here truth and beauty are deemed dangerous, as they make society inefficient and slow:

> Universal happiness keeps the wheels steadily turning, truth and beauty can't. (Huxley 1932)

Just because we're used to the Internet, online games, and social platforms, we hardly feel that we're delegated to a State "indentured" happiness. Nonetheless, contemporary digital behavioral design has us chasing the next dopamine kick while bombarding us with distractions on a daily basis. The idea that the private is public and "everything belongs to everybody" is not only knit into the fabric of the regime portrayed in Huxley's novel, it is also an integral component of social platforms. An example is Snapchat's function, Snap Map, that via location tracking gives Snapchat-friends the option to see where you are, if you're single, in a relationship or married; harvest more likes if your profile on Instagram, TikTok or Facebook is open and accessible to all users. To further unearth tech platforms' use of behavioral surveillance and means of constructing public spaces, we need to dust off another dystopian novel from the bookshelf, namely George Orwell's masterpiece *1984,* from 1949. In *1984,* there is a ministry responsible for propaganda, historical revisionism, culture and entertainment. As with the other Ministries in the state of Oceania, the name is naturally a misnomer, as the main purpose of this particular ministry is exactly propaganda, misinformation and rewriting historical events so they align with the wishes and opinions of Big Brother. It is a place where lies are manufactured and it's called 'The Ministry of Truth'.

The analogy is not that the purpose of social platforms and other online services is to produce lies, bullshit, fake news and misinformation as in Oceania's The Ministry of Truth. The analogy is that social platforms and BigTech originally made bandwidth, networks, search options and product variants of golf balls and knickknacks widely and readily available to consumers. An added bonus of the great catalogue of offers, is that our attention is something that imperceptibly can be controlled and directed like a projector's beam of light, and that we, and not the least those who manage and control the available information and its infrastructure, can turn up or dim the light, adjust where it shines and virtually focus or rearrange the entire lighting of the stage of attention, at will—a potent means of information control.

Deprivation of freedom and pervasive monitoring, with the illusion that free will and autonomy are still intact, begs the question—does the integration of the casino industry and surveillance capitalism define the state of social platforms? The contemporary horror scenario is that digitization and the Internet have enabled the collection of such a massive amount of data on human behavior that surveillance can become omnipresent and leave us with nowhere to hide. The doomsday version of a systematic deprivation of free will and a complete modification of behavior, so that it aligns with the wills and wants of a particular system, requires comprehensive mass surveillance.

In the legendary description of Las Vegas in Martin Scorsese's epic movie *Casino*, the high-rolling gambler and casino executive Sam "Ace" Rothstein, played by American actor Robert De Niro, aptly summarizes the surveillance of the gambler and casino employees:

> In Vegas, everybody's gotta watch everybody else (…) the dealers are watching the players. The box men are watching the dealers. The floor men are watching the box men. The pit bosses are watching the floor men. The shift bosses are watching the pit bosses. The casino manager is watching the shift bosses. I'm watching the casino manager. And the eye-in-the-sky is watching us all.

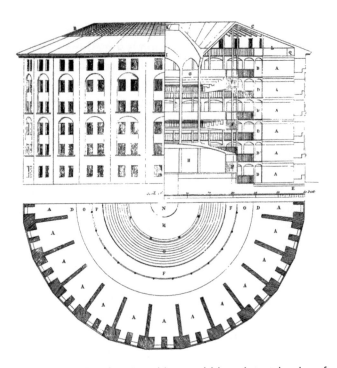

Fig. 6.3 Jeremy Benthem's architectural blueprint and guise of a prison, where the imprisoned are subject to constant surveillance and have nowhere to hide from the gaze of guards in their cells (Wikipedia Commons, verified 25.01.2021: https://commons.wikimedia.org/wiki/File:Penetentiary_Panopticon_Plan.jpg)

This may sound like the British philosopher Jeremy Bentham's (1748–1832) *panopticon* (all seeing), a place where the eyes of others always rest on the back of your head. Every life is surveilled around the clock, under the piercing gaze of the authorities and devoid of privacy. Privacy in the panopticon is simply not possible (Fig. 6.3).

The panopticon makes use of surveillance to discipline the inmates into conforming to the desired behavior. Or as

Bentham states:" *The more* strictly *we* are watched, the *better we behave.*"[15] Surveillance contributes to a disciplining of the surveilled (Haidt 2012). The information that follows surveillance takes on a disciplinary form of power (Foucault 1979). Regardless of whether surveillance is carried out in institutions such as prisons, schools, hospitals, the workplace, in the army or broadly applied to society as a whole, the aim is the same—to produce obedient and law abiding citizens who adapt to and follow the wants and expectations of authorities.

Digital surveillance and data collection are efficient tools for affecting behavioral change and regulation when combined with an appropriate reward and sanction structure for desirable and undesirable behavior. China makes use of this panoptic technique to further its ambition of disciplining its citizens (Hendricks & Vestergaard 2019, Vestergaard 2019). The regime's credit system is reminiscent of an Orwellian dystopia, where the regime exacts controls on citizen behavior through rewards and punishment—now with due assistance from big data as a kind of Big Brother and digital panopticon.

By monitoring and collecting data from social platform behavior, CCTV cameras, public and private databases and the like, those who conform to the desirable behavior as defined by the regime are awarded social credits that can provide a Chinese citizen with socio-economic advantages ranging from travel opportunities and favorable loans to cheaper utility bills, etc. For example, doing a good deed for a relative who needs help can generate points. On the other hand, if you exhibit undesirable behavior e.g., by speeding, the regime punishes you by subtracting social credit points, thereby

---

[15] From Jeremy Benthams manuscripts, Library of University College London. *Leaflets on Bentham's Life and Work*, verified 01.25.2021: https://www.ucl.ac.uk/bentham-project/publications/leaflets-benthams-life-and-work

limiting your options. It's new citizen management (Vestergaard 2019).

Beijing is not Silicon Valley, and a casino is not a panopticon. They do, however, share a lot of similarities. BigTech harvest and analyze data, including data from citizens in liberal democracies, on such a scale, that they can be utilized to change the behaviors and habits of people. Even the free Western world has seen alliances between the tech-industry and authorities in framing security policy issues where the mass surveillance of social platform users was an integrated part of the (espionage-) package, as documented by whistle-blower Edward Snowden (Snowden 2019).[16]

Now that social platforms have become an integral part of the global critical infrastructure, they have initiated expansive and often opaque editorial and content moderation practices that can quickly make them into that which they decisively, and self-proclaimed, do not want to be—'arbiters of truth'. The truth is not least an appropriate tool for things to work and systems to function. Or as Orwell writes in *1984*:

> In philosophy, or religion, or ethics, or politics, two and two might make five, but when one was designing a gun or an aeroplane they had to make four. (Orwell 1949): 32

Huxley and Orwell capture, in each their own way, where tech-platforms might take us. Huxley's and Orwell's novels are overlapping warnings of a world where the Soma-regime and Big Brother control facts, emotions and narratives. Today, unlike in *1984*, Big Brother doesn't just peer at us. No—we also choose to look to Big Brother, in hope of

---

[16] Biddle, S. (2017). "How Peter Thiel's Palentir Helped the NSA spy on the Whole World", *The Intercept*, 22.02.2017, verified 25.01.2021: https://theintercept.com/2017/02/22/how-peter-thiels-palantir-helped-the-nsa-spy-on-the-whole-world/

finding likes, lightness and happiness on the information super highway. As Neil Postman so brilliantly and lyrically summarizes in the foreword to *Amusing Ourselves to Death* from 1985:

> What Orwell feared were those who would ban books. What Huxley feared was that there would be no reason to ban a book, for there would be no one who wanted to read one. Orwell feared those who would deprive us of information. Huxley feared those who would give us so much that we would be reduced to passivity and egoism. Orwell feared that the truth would be concealed from us. Huxley feared the truth would be drowned in a sea of irrelevance. Orwell feared we would become a captive culture. Huxley feared we would become a trivial culture, preoccupied with some equivalent of the feelies, the orgy porgy, and the centrifugal bumblepuppy. (…) In short, Orwell feared that what we hate will ruin us. Huxley feared that what we love will ruin us. (Postman 1985): 23

7

Arbiters of Truth

"I don't think that Facebook or Internet platforms in general should be arbiters of truth."

– Mark Zuckerberg

It may very well be that the intention or ambition of social platforms and BigTech isn't to act as *arbiters of truth*. Arbiters, determining what is true or false, issue by issue, or deciders of which voices and stories find their way into the light cone of a platform's attention projector.

Nevertheless, the platforms routinely end up with a considerable part of exactly that responsibility in terms of granting access to current and historical events, rule and reign over news feeds and exchanges of opinions and altercations, allocation of attention and accordingly control of critical infrastructure, the personal and public space and democratic dialogue. Platforms largely decide what gets attention—and may even act as supranational institutions that command enormous influence on the information stream nationally and internationally. This potent position is decisive for how public discourse is informed and how democracy is stimulated and maintained—online and offline.

© The Author(s), under exclusive license to Springer Nature Switzerland AG 2022
V. F. Hendricks, C. Mehlsen, *The Ministry of Truth*,
https://doi.org/10.1007/978-3-030-98629-2_7

7.1   Shutting Down the News Stream

A social platform's declared *raison d'etre*, granting citizens and users around the world access to information, may be at odds with the platform's business model. This happened when Facebook, in a rather activistic way, decided to close an entire country's newsfeed.

On February 17, 2021 in an erupting feud between Facebook and the Australian government, Facebook decided to bar its users from finding and sharing news articles on Facebook. It was the most far-reaching action that the world's largest content provider to date had exercised against other content providers. The background for the action was an Australian bill that required tech platforms to pay news services for the content shown on their platforms.

When users read and share news on social platforms it generates traffic, and traffic generates data that may be analyzed, curated and sold or rented to advertisers who have a desire to advertise their products to a specific subset of the population. News is an information product, and yet again, Facebook earns money on the news that the global media—from *Le Monde* and *Frankfurter Allgemeine* to *The New York Times* and *The Guardian*—choose to link to the platform. According to Campbell Brown, Facebook's vice president for Global News Partnerships, it is the news media themselves that choose to share their stories on Facebook.[1] William Easton, Facebook's managing director and VP for Australia og New Zealand also claimed that with its bill, the Australian government had failed to acknowledge the economic benefits to the press and established media: Because they can sell more subscriptions, increase their readership and advertisement intake, "the value exchange between Facebook and

---

[1] Brown, C. (2021). "The Value of News on Facebook", Facebook, 02.17.2021, verified   06.05.2021:   https://www.facebook.com/journalismproject/news-australia-decision

publishers runs in favor of the publishers — which is the reverse of what the legislation would require the arbitrator to assume." According to Facebook, news accounts for less than 4% of the total content that users see, which is why news makes up only a small part of Facebook's total business.[2]

From the press' perspective, the case looks without reservation quite different. In Australia, Google alone is responsible for 53% of all online ads while the other, Facebook, commands 28%, and the remainder is shared here and there between smaller players.[3] At the same time almost 40% of Australians got their news from Facebook in the years from 2018 to 2020.[4] Something similar is seen with Americans,[5] while the numbers in Europe range from 45% in Italy to 22% in Germany during 2016–2020.[6]

Younger generations especially use social platforms as their news channels. Facebook, for example, is the largest news source for young Danes: 75% of Danish high school students gather their news from Facebook, while 57% of students get it from Instagram, e.g. on a weekly basis, 57% of Danish high school students have used Facebook for news or information about Covid-19 (Mehlsen 2020).

---

[2] Easton, W. (2021). "Changes to Sharing and Viewing News on Facebook in Australia", Facebook, 02.17.2021, verified 06.05.2021: https://about.fb.com/news/2021/02/changes-to-sharing-and-viewing-news-on-facebook-in-australia/

[3] BBC (2021). "Australia news code: What's this row with Facebook and Google all about?", BBC, 02.18.2021, verified 06.05.2021: https://www.bbc.com/news/world-australia-56107028

[4] BBC (2021). "Facebook Australia row: How Facebook became so powerful in news", BBC, 02.18.2021, verified 06.05.2021: https://www.bbc.com/news/world-australia-56109580

[5] Gramlich, J. (2021). "10 facts about Americans and Facebook", Pew Rersearch Center, 06.01.2021, verified 06.05.2021: https://www.pewresearch.org/fact-tank/2021/06/01/facts-about-americans-and-facebook/

[6] Watson, A. (2021). "Share of news consumers who used Facebook for news in European countries from 2016 to 2020", Statista, 04.27.2021, verified 06.05.2021: https://www.statista.com/statistics/298038/platforms-used-to-share-online-news-uk/

Google and Facebook sit on a virtual news monopoly—both in terms of distribution and advertising revenue. This is precisely the argument that Australia used for adopting its bill. Similar initiatives are being considered or are already instigated in other countries around the World. After Facebook shut down the newsfeed to 17 million Australian users, the firm came to an agreement with the Australian government and announced that the platform from there on out would work more closely with the government in deciding which news media may appear on Facebook.[7]

Facebook and Google agreed to pay for news in Australia, but Microsoft, who operates Bing, the search engine accounting for 5% of the global search market, from the outset expressed support for the Australian government's legislation.[8] Countries around the world and the World Trade Organization (WTO) are anxiously waiting to see whether such agreements will set a clear precedent for news partnerships between the news media and tech platforms. A problem, may however quickly evolve to the effect that only the largest news organizations are able to enter into such agreements, which may lead to even greater non-transparent concentrations of power between giant corporations, new and old. Size matters.

---

[7] Easton, W. (2021). "Changes to Sharing and Viewing News on Facebook in Australia", Facebook, 02.17.2021, verified 06.05.2021: https://about.fb.com/news/2021/02/changes-to-sharing-and-viewing-news-on-facebook-in-australia/

[8] Porter, J. (2021). "Australia passes law requiring Facebook and Google to pay for news content", *The Verge*, 02.24.2021, verified 06.05.22021: https://www.theverge.com/2021/2/24/22283777/australia-new-media-bargaining-code-facebook-google-paying-news

7.2   "Don't be Evil"

Google.com is the most visited website on the entire Internet; thus, it isn't surprising that it holds 88% of the search engine market. Google has a long list of other information products in its portfolio—products whose names all start with Google: Docs, Sheets, Slides, Translate, Scholar, Chat, Podcasts, Chrome, Maps, Waze, Earth, Street View, ranging all the way from the mail client Gmail to information related hardware products like Google Pixel, Home, Wifi and not the least, the virtual reality goggles Google Daydream.[9]

Google, which was founded in 1998 by two computer scientists, Larry Page and Sergey Brin, while still PhD students at Stanford University, has grown to be one of the world's most valuable companies. Starting out, Google wasn't funded by advertisements. Page and Brin had the ambition to offer the ultimately best search engine for free and without hidden business methods, concealed advertisement architectures or exploitations of users like the systems the competing search engines at the time were based on. In conjunction with Google's initial public offering (IPO) in 2004, the two founders published an unsubtle critique of its competitors, which came to be known as the *Don't Be Evil* manifesto:

> Don't be evil. We believe strongly that in the long term, we will be better served—as shareholders and in all other ways—by a company that does good things for the world even if we forgo some short term gains.[10]

---

[9] Alexa (2021). "The top 500 sites on the web", *Alexa.com*, verified 07.06.2021: https://www.alexa.com/topsites Statista (2021)."

Worldwide desktop market share of leading search engines from January 2010 to February 2021", *Statista.com*, verified 06.07.2021: https://www.statista.com/statistics/216573/worldwide-market-share-of-search-engines/

[10] Ovide, S. (2011). "Google's "Don't Be Evil" No Longer Prefaces Code of Conduct", *Search Engine Journal*, 05.20.2021, verified 06.07.2021: https://www.wsj.com/articles/BL-DLB-33777

However, many often forget that Google, in 2004, was among the first companies to implement a surveillance capitalism business model based on user data analysis and market segmented advertising campaigns. This was also why the company's profits rose by 3.590% from 86 million dollars in 2001 to 3.2 billion dollars in 2004 (Zuboff 2019a). "Don't be evil" was originally included in the preface to Google's "Code of Conduct" but in 2008 it was relegated to the very last sentence and now reads, "And remember…don't be evil, and if you see something that you think isn't right — speak up."[11] In 2013, Eric Schmidt, Google's former CEO from 2001–2011, confessed that he thought "Don't be evil" was stupid.[12] Around the same, while still head of Google, Schmidt was also quoted saying, in quintessential dystopian control style:

> I actually think most people don't want Google to answer their questions, they want Google to tell them what they should be doing next.[13]

Several current and former employees have held Google to its word when they saw something that wasn't right: They have launched criticism of Google along multiple axes; from poor work environment, gender and race discrimination, questionable ethics concerning the use of artificial intelligence, lack of transparency in operations, top-down management, market dominance distorting healthy competition,

---

[11] DailyTech (2013). "*Google's Eric Schmidt: "Don't Be Evil" was Stupid*", *DailyTech*, 05.14.2013, verified 06.07.2021: https://www.searchenginejournal.com/google-dont-be-evil/254019/#close

[12] Jenkins, H.W. (2010). "Google and the Search for the Future", *Wall Street Journal*, 08.14.2020, verified 06.22.2021: http://www.dailytech.com/Googles+Eric+Schmidt+Dont+Be+Evil+was+Stupid/article31544.htm

[13] Jenkins, H.W. (2010). "Google and the Search for the Future", *Wall Street Journal*, 08.14.2020, verified 06.22.2021: https://www.wsj.com/articles/SB10001424052748704901104575423294099527212

inconsistent content moderation and last but not least, a pronounced *bias* in Google's search algorithms and results.[14]

There isn't unequivocal evidence for some particular political bias or bias towards specific groups, demographics, events or news sources in Google's algorithmic search structure. But there is clear evidence for bias generated by Google's (and YouTube's) recommender-based systems, which reproduces the Matthew effect: To those that have, more will be given.

Google uses software that constantly monitors and trawls the web for new information shared online. This information is indexed, categorized and saved on Google's server network. The next time a user initiates a search—for example "the consequences of the 2021 Capitol riots"—Google will consequently know what information is available on this specific topic. To make sure that the search results are as relevant as possible at a given time, Google uses a number of algorithms that take into consideration factors such as word choice, traffic, user friendliness, source trustworthiness, the user's geographic location, settings and search history.[15] What is quite crucial is the website's *authoritative status*, which Google determines by a number of factors, such as the number of inbound links from other websites and how authoritative these other sites are themselves. It is self-reinforcing, in the sense that Google considers a website authoritative, if it is already authoritative.

The weekly magazine, *The Economist*, undertook a statistical study that found that Google searches more frequently reward reputable and accurate reporting over left-wing politics. To determine the accuracy of a publication or news story

[14] Elias, J. (2020). "Google researcher's dismissal is a perfect storm for employee unrest — and a big test for CEO Sundar Pichai", *CNBC*, 12.08.2020, verified 06.07.2021: https://www.cnbc.com/2020/12/08/timnit-gebru-departure-perfect-storm-for-alphabet-ceo-sundar-pichai.html

[15] Google (2021). "How Search algorithms work", *Google.com*, verified 06.07.2021: https://www.google.com/search/howsearchworks/algorithms/

The Economist explored how the story was classified by fact-checker institutions, how many Pulitzer-prize winners they had on staff (if any) and how the respective portals ranked on YouGovs American news media trustworthiness poll.

It may sound like a sober method, but as *The Economist* noted: "If fact-checkers and Pulitzer prizewinners are partisan, our model will be too,"[16] which again is a testimony to the systematic bias in Google searches. If you do not consider widely trusted news media to be reputable or authoritative, you won't rely heavily on Google search results. Google searches may certainly be biased, but bias will then be a reward of a Matthew effect related to degree of engagement, traffic and interest, where one's interest is determined by geolocation and personal search history. (Vaidhyanathan 2012).

Bias via the Matthew effect is still bias—and when the 5.4 billion searches handled by Google every day[17] are taken into account, Google becomes the global content manager of information searches and inevitably an arbiter of truth.

7.3   Public Space on Private Hands

On October 23, 2019, democratic congresswomen Alexanderia Ocasia-Cortez (AOC) got Facebook's founder and director, Mark Zuckerberg, to admit that one could indeed buy one's way to misinformation campaigns on Facebook. A week after Zuckerberg's admission, something happened on another social platform—Twitter. Twitter's co-founder, Jack Dorsey, announced a ban on political

[16] *The Economist* (2019). "Google rewards reputable reporting, not left-wing politics", 08.06.2019, verified 11.01.2022: https://www.economist.com/graphic-detail/2019/06/08/google-rewards-reputable-reporting-not-left-wing-politics

[17] Georgiev, D. (2021). "111+ Google Statistics and Facts That Reveal Everything About the Tech Giant", *Review 42*, 10.12.2021, verified 11.01.2022: https://review42.com/resources/google-statistics-and-facts/

marketing across all of Twitter. Dorsey's announcement was made through a series of tweets, of an almost Kantian inspiration, forming one single categorical imperative and nine submaxims, which are now known as "Jack Dorsey's 10 theses" (Fig. 7.1):

Fig. 7.1 A selection of Jack Dorsey's 10 theses on Twitter, October 30, 2019

> We've made the decision to stop all political advertising on Twitter globally. We believe political message reach should be earned, not bought. Why? A few reasons…[18]

This imperative is followed by the submaxims, which point out among other things,

1. the reach of a political message is something that should be earned, not bought,
2. powerful political advertising may drive voters in unfortunate directions and affect millions of lives,
3. political marketing on the internet presents whole new challenges, for the public debate and for democracy, because of the potential for micro-segmentation of voter groups, misinformation and deep fakes,
4. there is a need for more regulation in the area of political ads.

The tenth and final thesis addresses the question that has long been the subject of public debate—social platforms and their relationship to the central democratic value of freedom of expression:

> A final note. This isn't about free expression. This is about paying for reach. And paying to increase the reach of political speech has significant ramifications that today's democratic infrastructure may not be prepared to handle. It's worth stepping back in order to address.

The social platforms are private companies, which own everything from the users' profiles to the generated content. If you can't agree to the platforms' terms of use, you can just

---

[18] Dorsey, J. (2019). "A political message earns reach when people decide to follow an account or retweet …", Twitter, 10.30.2019, verified 06.07.2021: https://twitter.com/jack/status/1189634367296901120

create your own server and broadcast to the world. But as influencer Anders Hemmingsen having over a million followers on Instagram, formulates the problem:

> If you were to rebel against it, then you would have to start your own app, your own platform, your own Facebook and own places where you would have to get people to go, and that is an impossible task since they are all bound to Facebook. (Mehlsen 2020)

If platforms remove a post or video, the argument is typically that it isn't a violation of free speech since you can just find another place to express yourself. However, the platforms of private companies have become so big and constitute such a large part of the public space and infrastructure—where opinions are voiced and democracy lives, that they have gained an almost monopoly-like power (Lauritzen & Stjernfelt 2018).

In the age of information, public space should be understood as a special *information structure* rather than a physical entrance criterium to a space, a town hall or other places, which historically have been perceived as public spaces (Hendricks & Hansen 2016). Public spaces constitute a fundamental base for democracy. With unlimited access to a centrally located public space, comes freedom and the ability for as many people as possible to share information and ideas in a way that incorporates them into society's collective consciousness.

In modern democracy, public spaces play a constant and fundamental democratic role in the provision of mutual recognition between citizens. In these public spaces, physical presence alone may lead to mutual recognition—the simple physical representation of the whole of society's citizens, in all their forms and appearances, establishes a public signal which inscribes itself in our collective consciousness. Society women with fanciful hats, the homeless on their cardboard boxes, children acting up, elderly with walking frames, sweaty school teachers with kids chasing pigeons, yuppies sipping cocktails, students with blue lit faces from Instagram's reflection glare and workers with their raw fists wrapped around hotdogs—they all have a right to a place in this consciousness. We are all represented through our collective consciousness and common background knowledge, as these form the basic premises for a democratic debate the framework of which is based on equality, freedom and mutual respect. The common value of public space is a fundamental value for democracy, whether we think of the City Hall Square in New York City or the steps of the Lincoln Memorial that provided the backdrop for "I Have a Dream".

When public space serves as a fundamental democratic pillar, it is a central premise that no one may claim special interest in or capitalize from it, as it would no longer be equal for all nor provide equal access. The past 15–20 years have has seen a paradigm shift in our understanding and ownership of the public space. In conjunction with public space increasingly becoming digital infrastructure, our temporal physical presence in the same physical space has become less important.

It is not democratic nations or supranational organizations that have facilitated this massive transformation of public space, but private enterprise and primarily BigTech such as Google, YouTube, Amazon, Microsoft, Apple and not least Meta/Facebook running the world's largest town hall with one third of the global population. These tech companies however do not answer to the founding democratic principles, but instead to their advertisers and stockholders.

It may very well be that all citizens have gained a voice, in so far that virtually anyone can have a profile on a social platform. What is of interest however, is not that we've all gained a voice but whether our voice is heard. Some people and some things are heard and seen more than others in the information market ruled by the attention economy; hence some privileged parties have a greater possibility of becoming part of our collective consciousness.

Much may be said about democracies but they've seldom, if ever, been decidedly pecuniary profitable. Democracy is the societal model that we in the Western world have thought of as the pre-eminent way of serving both individual and collective interests. With the dominance of BigTech it's worth asking whether public space should be left to private enterprise—or if it in reverse is downright detrimental to the individual as well the collective?

Had we once again consulted Kant, Rousseau or Montesquieu, who contributed to carving out the philosophical path for democracy during the Enlightenment, whether the infrastructure of public space should be on private hands, their answer would have been a firm and resounding—no thanks! There can't be special interest and no one should be able to capitalize on the democratic infrastructure if the marketplace of free ideas is exactly to be free and equally accessible to all.

7.4   Everything but Water

There is a reason why national road systems in liberal democracies more often than not are owned and administered by the state—everybody should be able to access this critical infrastructure on equal terms (Hendricks 2022). Traditionally this way of thinking has also governed national telecommunication networks typically installed, controlled and used by private companies or governments or some combination thereof to ensure customers/citizens have equal access to this critical infrastructure. This may however be an arrangement of the past. BigTech is exceedingly in the business of laying fiber-optic cables across continents as fiber-optics are carrying 95% of the global internet traffic—on route in some 1.3 million kilometers of bundled glass threads literally making up the physical internet. In less than 10 years Microsoft, Google, Meta and Amazon have become the dominant users of the undersea fiber-optics capacity—around 66%. In the years to come these four BigTech companies are projected to become the major financiers and thus owners of the submarine cable network and by 2024 it is estimated they will jointly own and run some 30 long-distance cables across the globe as compared to but one such conglomerate cable in 2010.[19]

In response to these projections traditional telecom companies and independent telecommunication analysts have voiced concerns about the societal, political and financial desirability of BigTech also owning the infrastructure in which they are offering their products and services. Thus, counting among their possessions not only owning the cars running on streets, but the streets themselves together with controlling the traffic lights and finally owning billboards and the stores passing your way. That's virtually laying claim to, owning and exercising executive power over the entire internet.[20] BigTech's involvement in the cable-laying industry has had the advantage of driving down costs of data transmission across the globe—partners and competitors alike—and increased the world's capacity to transmit data by

---

[19] Mims, C. (2022). "Google, Amazon, Meta and Microsoft Weave a Fiber-Optic Web of Power", *The Wall Street Journal*, 15.01.2022, verified 20.01.2022: https://www.wsj.com/articles/google-amazon-meta-and-microsoft-weave-a-fiber-optic-web-of-power-11642222824

[20] Cooper, T. (2019). "Google and other tech giants are quietly buying up the most important part of the internet", *Venturebeat*, 06.04.2019, verified 20.01.2022: https://venturebeat.com/2019/04/06/google-and-other-tech-giants-are-quietly-buying-up-the-most-important-part-of-the-internet/

40% in 2020 alone.[21] That's immediately good for business growth as well as user experience. Be that as it may, running cables and data centers requires power—lots of power especially for servers and cooling systems—so one could easily imagine BigTech being acutely interested in having their own energy supply making them less dependent on the national electrical grids they are currently tapping into worldwide and accordingly paying for power from third party supplier. But the energy sector is yet another part of critical infrastructure—so what's next? Taking stock of inventory it seems as if BigTech already have their fingers deep in the dial of critical infrastructure including *data and cloud, space, food and grocery, education, research and innovation, communications, transport, space, defence and national security, banking and finance*, even *health* … leaving just *water* to its own devices … so far (Fig. 7.2).

This is not to say that BigTech axiomatically entertains the ambition of worldwide domination in every sector of critical infrastructure. All the same, one thing tends to lead to another also without malignant or megalomaniac intent necessarily, so don't count your chickens quite yet. This spells yet another reason for careful contemplation, including regulatory reform and reflective regulation. On a smaller scale BigTech has already been seen to exercise their executive power resorting to rather drastic measures when it comes to the democratically elected and the critical democratic infrastructure of public space.

This is exactly where January 7th, 2021, Deplatforming Day, represents a landmark event in more ways than one. It was a landmark event because BigTech used an unprecedented decommissioning strategy to shut down Trump after

---

[21] Mims, C. (2022). "Google, Amazon, Meta and Microsoft Weave a Fiber-Optic Web of Power", The Wall Street Journal, 15.01.2022, verified 20.01.2022: https://www.wsj.com/articles/google-amazon-meta-and-microsoft-weave-a-fiber-optic-web-of-power-11642222824

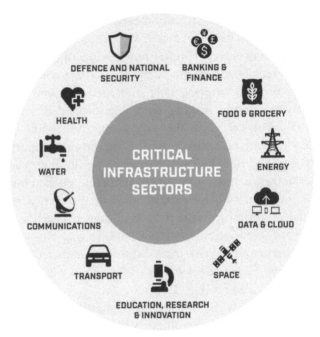

Fig. 7.2   The dial of critical infrastructure

the Capitol siege. Why did BigTech choose a decommissioning strategy at exactly this point in time? Had they suddenly changed their minds after Congress was breached? Do they acknowledge a social responsibility for the democratic infrastructure? Is it because they can hear Fenrir, the monstrous *wolf* of Norse mythology, howling about regulatory and legislative interventions? Or do they want to be on the "right side of history"? Even the history books will probably not provide a clear-cut answer.

Nonetheless Deplatforming Day laid bare that social platforms decide who has access to an essential part of democracy's public space—and that they henceforth are constitutive in restructuring the premises of the public sphere and political conversation.

After the riots at the congressional building, Twitter permanently banned Trump, a democratically elected president, from its platform. Facebook initially chose to exclude Trump until after the official transition of power to the newly elected Biden-Harris administration. In the meantime Facebook's Oversight Board for Content was tasked to specifically deal with the exclusion of Trump.[22]

Facebook's Oversight Board for Content founded in 2019, consists of 20 experts from around the world. These experts are paid for their work by an independent foundation, established and financed by Meta/Facebook, in order to secure an arm's length principle. The purpose of the Board is to make independent and binding decisions on principal cases and questions related to censorship and the criteria of content moderation on Facebook and Instagram. Facebook has called its Oversight Board the "supreme court" of content affairs.[23] The supreme court can issue rulings on specific cases and determine general guidelines for content moderation that are more or less binding for Facebook.

On May 25th, 2021 the Oversight Board announced its long awaited "ruling" over Facebook's decision to cancel the 45th president of the United States, Donald J. Trump's Facebook and Instagram accounts. The Oversight Board reasoned that even though it was due diligence to suspend Trump's account at a time when the president had incited unrest and instigated a siege of the Capitol, there was not necessarily anything that could justify an indefinite ban from the platform. The decision was then sent back to Facebook

---

[22] Facebook (2019). "Facebook Oversight Board for Content Decisions: What to Know", Facebook, 08.22.2019, verified 06.07.2021: https://www.facebook.com/journalismproject/facebook-oversight-board-for-content-decisions-overview

[23] Klonick, K. (2021). "Inside the Making of Facebook's Supreme Court", *The New Yorker*, 12.02.2021, verified 08.08.2021: https://www.newyorker.com/tech/annals-of-technology/inside-the-making-of-facebooks-supreme-court

by the Oversight Board with a recommendation to either retain the suspension indefinitely or reactivate Trump's account after 6 months—and under any circumstance, Facebook should return with a catalogue of clear and transparent rules explaining the rationale for their decision and a general but rigorous procedure that may be applied going forward.[24]

After a month Facebook returned to the Oversight Board with a decision to uphold Trump's suspension from Facebook and Instagram for a period of 2 years and at the end of the period evaluate with a team of experts whether public safety and order once again has returned to a level where Trump's Facebook and Instagram accounts can be reactivated and opened to traffic. Meta/Facebook is to determine whether public safety and public order are in such a state that Trump may regain his accounts, sounds as if the company is to make determinations which in liberal democracies normally file under the police authorities and legislative body.

Along with the ongoing ban, Facebook submitted a protocol explaining the general guidelines and "penalties" to be leveraged on public figures on the platforms, in times of civil unrest and violent riots (Fig. 7.3). The protocol also contains statements about responsibility and transparency in conjunction with Facebook's and Instagram's so called "strike system", where users may be excluded from the platform through a point system, as well as an explanation of a regulatory "newsworthy allowance" for news that would otherwise run counter to the community standards, which seldomly nevertheless may be upheld on the platform if Facebook deems it relevant to public interests.[25]

---

[24] Dwoskin, E. & Zakrzewski, C. (2021). "Facebook's Oversight Board upholds ban on Trump. At least for now", *Washington Post*, 05.05.2021, verified 08.07.2021

[25] Clegg, N. (2021). "In Response to Oversight Board, Trump Suspended for Two Years; Will Only Be Reinstated if Conditions Permit", Facebook, 04.06.2021,

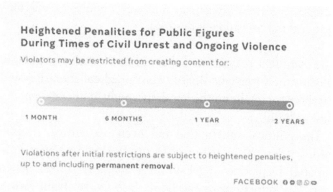

Fig. 7.3 Quarantine sanctions for public figures on Facebook and Instagram

The entirety of the catalogue was given to the Oversight Board by Nick Clegg, Vice President of Global Affairs at Facebook. The response ended with a comment that, on the one hand, not only cemented Facebook's massive power over the democratic infrastructure but also the company willingness to take matters into their own hands and define their own global protocols in a time when the political system didn't; and, on the other hand, made an appeal for more legislation in these matters:

> It's response to this case confirms our view that Facebook shouldn't be making so many decisions about content by ourselves. In the absence of frameworks agreed upon by democratically accountable lawmakers, the board's model of independent and thoughtful deliberation is a strong one that ensures important decisions are made in as transparent and judicious a manner as possible. The Oversight Board is not a

---

verified 08.06.2021: https://about.fb.com/news/2021/06/facebook-response-to-oversight-board-recommendations-trump/

replacement for regulation, and we continue to call for thoughtful regulation in this space.[26]

The comment may be read that either the task of regulation falls on the Oversight Board's continued collaboration with Facebook or it falls on the legislative body of liberal democracies, or both …

The political system that has been inattentive, sleeping through class, has finally woken up. In the first senate hearing after Deplatforming Day on March 25th, 2021, where Mark Zuckerberg from Facebook, Jack Dorsey from Twitter and Sundar Pichai from Google took the stand, the politicians had done their homework and now understood the seriousness of the increasing influence tech platforms have on facts, feelings and fictions … and the state of democracy in the information age.[27] The question remains: What now?!

---

[26] Ibid. Clegg (2021).

[27] Fung, B. (2021). "Facebook, Twitter and Google CEOs grilled by Congress on misinformation", *CNN*, 25.05.2021, verified 08.06.2021: https://edition.cnn.com/2021/03/25/tech/tech-ceos-hearing/index.html

8

What Now?!

"That's why we need to keep taking firm action against dominant companies that misuse their power, to drive smaller, innovative rivals out of the market. Because dominant companies are too often champions gone wrong – champions that seek to fend off rivals and protect their position. So stopping those companies from abusing their power has been a priority for several years now – and the pandemic hasn't slowed it down at all."

– Margrethe Vestager, 2021 (European Commissioner for Competition)

Time and again it may seem too little and too late—the lead of BigTech is simply too mammoth for us to catch up with. It all began at the end of the 1990s and the turn of the millennium with a vision of democratization, the sharing of innocent cat videos, friendly requests, networks and online queries for tapes, books and freezer chests and spare parts. It didn't take long for BigTech to discover the value of attention, the financial potential of a data-driven economy and the key to surveillance capitalism's business model. And where are we now—and where do we go from here individually, institutionally and ideologically?

© The Author(s), under exclusive license to Springer Nature Switzerland AG 2022
V. F. Hendricks, C. Mehlsen, *The Ministry of Truth*,
https://doi.org/10.1007/978-3-030-98629-2_8

8.1   Sober October

For Meta/Facebook—and the world at large—October 2021 was anything but a sober month, but if none other, a sobering experience. On October 4, 3.5 million users of Facebook, Instagram and WhatsApp got to experience firsthand how life is without the global information borne infrastructure provided by Meta. For some 6 h Facebook, Instagram and WhatsApp were down in what has since been labelled the Great (Facebook) Blackout.[1] The blackout made it abundantly clear that the public space of private persons and corporations alike is as fragile as it is privately owned and monopolized.

Facebook set to sea in 2004 and acquired subsequently the image sharing service Instagram in 2012 for $1 billion. Back then, Instagram employed measly 13 souls but was all the same considered a "threat" to Facebook by Zuckerberg.[2] Today, Instagram is approximately a 1 billion users strong and is responsible for about $20 billions of Meta's surplus. In 2014 Facebook bought WhatsApp the message service for a dizzying $19 billion—the reason—the same as before: There was a worry that WhatsApp might outcompete Meta/Facebook internally leaked documents showed back in 2018.[3]

The strategy for Meta/Facebook has been clear for long. Outcompete the competition by buying it up to acquire the monopoly—anything else is for losers as tech mogul Peter

[1] Smith, R. (2021). "On Surviving the Great Facebook Blackout of 2021", *Vogue*, 06.10.2021, verified 12.01.2022: https://www.vogue.com/article/on-surviving-the-great-facebook-blackout-of-2021

[2] Business Standard (2020). "Mark Zuckerberg bought Instagram as it was a 'threat' to Facebook", 30.06.2020, verified 12.01.2022: https://www.business-standard.com/article/international/mark-zuckerberg-bought-instagram-as-it-was-a-threat-to-facebook-120073000324_1.html

[3] Warzel, C. & Mac, R. (2018). "These Confidential Charts Show Why Facebook Bought WhatsApp", *BuzzFeed*, 05.12.2018, verified 12.01.2022: https://www.buzzfeednews.com/article/charliewarzel/why-facebook-bought-whatsapp

Thiel apparently taught his apprentice Mark Zuckerberg (Chafkin 2021). This is also the reason why the Federal Trade Commission (FTC) of the US on December 9, 2020 filed a lawsuit against Meta/Facebook for illegal monopolization due to the acquisitions of WhatsApp and Instagram.[4] Meta/Facebook asked for the case to be dropped which ironically happened the very same day as the Great Blackout.

Facebook, Instagram and WhatsApp were running as separate platforms until 2019 when they were united into one mastodon infrastructure with all the maintenance, data harvesting, advertising, profiling, forecasting, predicting and behavior modifying advantages the merger accordingly afforded. Users are fed the same story time and time again that it is good for the user experience, while deftly leaving out that it is even better still for the BigTech business model to have ever more integrated data about the users: The better we know you, the better we can sell you to the advertisers, and the longer you stay in the Meta-casino, the more attention you pay while generating more engagement and data boosting BigTech profits.

The advantages of merging Facebook, Instagram and WhatsApp into one comes at prize. Some glitch or error one place may swiftly propagate to the entire digital lattice leading all three services to an outage at the same time. Before you know it, it is not just about the ability to get in touch with your immediate network, send pictures and meme messages along getting hit by the Great Blackout, but about the entire infrastructure making the wheels turn for citizens, corporations, society and digital democracy.

The global interruption of services was caused by a connection command error between Meta/Facebook's backbone

---

[4] FTC (2020). "FTC Sues Facebook for Illegal Monopolization", Federal Trade Commission, 09.12.2020, verified 12.01.2022: https://www.ftc.gov/news-events/press-releases/2020/12/ftc-sues-facebook-illegal-monopolization

servers and the Internet according to company report.[5] The Great Blackout has been compared to a global power outage the timing of which hardly could be more unfortunate and annoying for the company.

The day before, October 3, a face was put to Meta/Facebook whistleblower "Sean", when Frances Haugen appeared on CBS *60 Minutes* with devasting criticism of the company all backed up meticulously by leaked internal documents. Haugen showed how Meta/Facebook systematically puts profits before people whether a matter of rolling back otherwise effective measures for blocking the proliferation of misinformation during a Presidential election or neglecting company conducted research about hazards and degeneration of mental health among youth by Instagram-usage to mention but a few of Haugen's charges.[6]

Then comes the Great Blackout on October 4. Then on October 5, 2021 Frances Haugen testifies before the United States Senate Committee on Commerce, Science and Transportation. Democrats and Republicans are horrified by what they hear pertaining to Meta/Facebook's knowledge that their own algorithms are stoking division, hurting people, weakening democracy; about structural problems of deliberate understaffing. Haugen also presented remedying suggestions for how the company should only go for chronological newsfeeds, generic advertising rather than targeted marketing and additionally install various friction strategies

[5] Janardhan, S. (2021). "More details about the October 4 outage, Facebook, 05.10.2021, verified 12.01.2022: https://engineering.fb.com/2021/10/05/networking-traffic/outage-details/

[6] A comprehensive list of the biggest revelations in the *Facebook Files* has been compiled by Danner, C. (2021). "What Is Being Leaked in the Facebook Papers: A guide to the biggest revelations.?", *The New York Magazine*, 27.10.2021, verified 17.01.2022: https://nymag.com/intelligencer/2021/10/what-was-leaked-in-the-facebook-papers.html

for users sharing information.[7] Her testimony certainly touched a nerve with Meta/Facebook where representatives scrambled to push back. Among them, company spokesman Andy Stone took to Twitter charging that Haugen was neither involved in child safety nor Instagram at her time in the company so how could she possibly know anything directly?[8] But the evidence she provided was harder to debunk especially as significant portions of it came from the company itself. CEO Mark Zuckerberg also fired back with a lengthy post on October 6, 2021 discrediting the Haugen statement and denying all allegations in a letter to employees that Zuckerberg subsequently made public.[9] Since then, Frances Haugen has testified before the British Parliament and the EU Parliament to give similar depositions,[10] appeared on multiple media shows and a constant presence in the press urging Mark Zuckerberg to step down[11]

Then on October 24, leaked additional documents from concerned employees at Meta/Facebook came to the light revealing that the company was well aware that its algorithmic architecture pushed users towards extreme content and polarization around the January 6 insurrection—and little

---

[7] Statement of Frances Haugen, October 4, 2021. United States Senate Committee on Commerce, Science and Transportation - Sub-Committee on Consumer Protection, Product Safety, and Data Security, verified 12.01.2022: https://www.commerce.senate.gov/services/files/FC8A558E-824E-4914-BEDB-3A7B1190BD49

[8] Andy Stone, Twitter, 05.10, 2021: https://twitter.com/andymstone/status/1445403468945055755

[9] Mark Zuckerberg, Facebook, 06.10.2021: https://www.facebook.com/zuck/posts/10113961365418581

[10] News – European Parliament – Press Release, 03.11.2021. "Facebook whistleblower Frances Haugen testifies in Parliament on 8 November", verified 12.01.2022: https://www.europarl.europa.eu/news/en/press-room/20211028IPR16121/facebook-whistleblower-frances-haugen-testifies-in-parliament-on-8-november

[11] Milmo, D. (2021). "Mark Zuckerberg should quit Facebook, says Frances Haugen", *The Guardian*, 01.11.2021, verified 12.01.2022: https://www.theguardian.com/technology/2021/nov/01/mark-zuckerberg-should-quit-facebook-says-frances-haugen

did the company do to stop the growth of conspiracy theories and conspiratorial group-think.[12] Fair to say that October 2021 was not a good month for Meta/Facebook but a sobering one for the rest of the world, citizens, businesses, politicians and lawmakers alike.

8.2   Mobilization

Citizens, politicians, governments, and supranational organizations, from the EU to the UN, have for long been sound asleep and lulled into the false premise that the development of digital platforms really and truly was just about spreading benign information, sharing knowledge, innovation, initiative, enterprise, enlightenment, empowerment, autonomy, freedom of expression, democracy and entertainment.

The world's politicians, leaders, and organizations were late to discover that BigTech had moved in and begun capitalizing and monopolizing virtually everything related to information, with attention and data at the nexus of their earnings—and in the age of information this literally means *everything*: news, videos, film, influencer culture, online gaming and a host of other entertainment packages, the marketplace of ideas, advertisements and public space, our critical infrastructure and the environments through which even liberal democracies live and breathe. Only in the final hour have we begun to examine how platforms align with competition legislation, taxation, copyrights, media responsibility, press ethics, privacy rights etc.

And now? BigTech has become so powerful that they can threaten to shut down a significant chunk of the news in an entire country if they so wish, potentially digitally colonize

---

[12] NBC News (2021). "Facebook Under Fire after New Documents Leaked", 24.10.2021, verified 17.01.2022: https://www.youtube.com/watch?v=FWvZLWjORFA

entire continents[13] and appropriate the guidelines of public discourse. Meta/Facebook might not be a nation, but it can mess with nations, as they've amassed sovereign control of critical infrastructure nearing all nations in the world have gradually come to depend on. The same goes for other mastodons, from Apple to Amazon.

On a rainy day it really seems that we've done too little, too late. On a sunny day, however, there is much we can do, both together and individually. It requires three types of mobilization to curtail the growing influence of BigTech on the public sphere and their ensuing power over the facts, emotions and narratives of our time:

1. Individual mobilization (as citizen and user)
2. Institutional mobilization (public, private, NGO)
3. Ideological mobilization (policy formation).

8.3   Individual Mobilization

The foundation of individual mobilization lies with *digital literacy*. Digital literacy means being able to understand, apply and be critical of digital technologies as well as to navigate and participate sustainably in digital communities (Mehlsen and Hendricks 2018). Digital literacy is likewise about understanding and being aware that our behavior is influenced by the way social platforms and digital services are designed.

No one may grow digitally literate without the interaction and influence of others. The conditions of social influence have not diminished on social platforms, rather it is the

---

[13] Marker, S.L., Vestergaard, M., Hendricks, V.F. (2018). "Digital colonialism on the African continent", *South African Business Report*, 16.10.2018, verified 08.07.2021: https://www.iol.co.za/business-report/opinion/opinion-digital-colonialism-on-the-african-continent-17493010

opposite. Online influence may spread with unprecedented ease and speed from person to person and groups across the globe.

Digital literacy refers to the *process* by which a person acquires the necessary knowledge and insight to be able to participate with self-determination and autonomy in a digitalized society. At the same time digital literacy also denotes the *result* of a process securing sustainable behaviors and norms both on and off the web.

Knowledge alone doesn't cut it—but theoretical knowledge coupled with the practical application strengthen one's critical faculty, agency and online empowerment. Digital literacy is to strengthen one's ability to sort online information and recognize structures that may lead to unsustainable social behaviors and thereby help us acquire collective and individual tools that we can use to resist engaging in unfortunate online social dynamics.

The task is to equip citizens with the ability to sort through the enormous amounts of online data they're exposed to on a daily basis and not least to strengthen their independent decision-making capabilities, autonomy and authority in a digital age where they soon will be the ones sitting by the end of the table calling the shots. All generations should be educated to understand the structure and dynamics of the information market and attention economy. Or as a student of ours has pointedly noted: "I don't think my parents are aware of the fact that they are the products" (Mehlsen and Hendricks 2019).

Children, youth and adults alike are all digital infants with the mere difference being that the challenges are age dependent. We all need to learn how to conduct ourselves online, sort information and resist the spreading of fake news and damaging content. Education is the most viable way of supporting critical capacities while strengthening our digital resilience to misinformation and online manipulation.

Since 2014, Finland has taken up the battle against fake news and armies of Russian trolls, partly by reforming its educational system to bolster critical online aptitudes and partly by developing educational initiatives aimed at the entire population. With a 1300 km shared border with Russia and Kremlin close at hand, Finland has endured Russian media propaganda for years. With propaganda moving online, preventative measures are increasingly centered on digital literacy. In schools and evening classes, students, citizens, journalists and politicians learn how to identify false profiles, bots, deep-fake videos etc. In developing a healthy democratic online culture it is imperative that citizens enhance their digital faculties and learn to identify the structures and mechanisms that support transgressive behavior.

8.4   Institutional Mobilization

Individual mobilization, digital literacy and education is not only a personal matter, it's also firmly tied to institutional mobilization. Whether it is public or private business or institutions and NGO's with the responsibility and ambition of engaging civil society, something that can be done on the institutional and corporate level much in the vein of Ethan Zuckerman's testimony:

> Increasingly, I'm inspired by entrepreneurs who run non-profit organizations that fund themselves, or for-profit organizations that achieve social missions while turning a profit.

An example that combines individual and institutional mobilization is WHO's 2020 initiative 'Social Media Listening', which attempts to immunize global populations from misinformation.[14] During the Covid-19 pandemic WHO have continuously collaborated with a data-analytics company to scrutinize the weekly 1.6 million pieces of Covid-19-related information on social platforms and divide these into four categories via a new health taxonomy, combined with artificial intelligence and machine learning: cause, disease, intervention and treatment. In doing so, WHO attained a more intricate understanding of the themes that were trending publicly and were thus better able to target its messaging on topics such as—When do you know that a pandemic is over? And how do you know when a new wave of coronavirus is about to break out?

Artificial intelligence may help determine user emotions through automated analysis of natural language, not merely as simple sentiment analysis in the form of positive, neutral and negative feelings, but by specifically identifying how emotions such as anxiety, anger, frustration, rejection or acceptance come to occupy certain themes in particular populations. One of the principles implemented by the Social Media Listening initiative, prioritizes speed over volume with the intent of uncovering the *virality of narratives* as opposed to the amount of information in circulation.

Lastly, and despite allegations of corrupt agendas and the danger of inciting mistrust and conspiracies, WHO remains principally impartial when it comes to passing judgement on which information is right or wrong. WHO seeks to share information the accuracy of which is verified by reliable sources. Here users play a salient role. Instead of thinking of citizens as passive sharers of information, the organization actively seeks to get us to search for dubious information that

---

[14] WHO (2020). "Immunizing the public against misinformation", 25.08.2020, verified 26.04.2021: https://www.who.int/news-room/feature-stories/detail/immunizing-the-public-against-misinformation

WHO may then factcheck and publish on its 'myth buster' page. Users are therefore able to take a more active stance on the pandemic and on the infodemic that's followed in its wake.

WHO and Facebook forged a partnership to fight misinformation during the first wave of the Covid-19 pandemic. An example of institutional mobilization where different agents—private and public collaborate—to address one or more global challenges.[15] Their partnership sets an example of how UN's 17th sustainable development goal (SDG), which essentially petitions institutions—private, public and NGO's—to enter into partnerships so that the 16 remaining SDGs may be addressed and realized. Rather than attempting to maximize utility individually and potentially get caught up in the prisoner's dilemma, we need more of this kind of institutional mobilization that animates us to collaborate for greater collective gains than what is possible to reach on an individual basis. That's the message of the stag hunt game—which exactly applies to the realization of the SDGs. The time is ripe to add a new UN SDG: *Sustainable Tech*.

A pressing question is how these macroscopic ambitions may be realized microscopically on a user level when, for example, dealing with misinformation and inappropriate information sharing in general.

Friction strategies are behavioral design measures that could make the production and proliferation of harmful content on social platforms quite cumbersome and time consuming—for humans as well as bots. Such strategies are

---

[15] Kang-Xing, J. (2021). "Reaching Billions of People With COVID-19 Vaccine Information", Facebook, 08.02.2021, verified 20.06.2021: https://about.fb.com/news/2021/02/reaching-billions-of-people-with-covid-19-vaccine-information/?_ga=2.132738887.818060407.1624189380-1196818519.1624189380

considered some of the most promising to battle subprime information products and bad behavior online.[16]

Friction may consist in micro-payments to be made by users for sharing or receiving information, or user-oriented mental expenditures through quizzes, puzzles or other micro-exams passed before user action is to commence. A concrete example tech platforms make use of already is CAPTCHA: **C**ompletely **A**utomated **P**ublic **T**uring test to tell **C**omputers and **H**umans **A**part. As digital gateways, CAPTCHAs may be easy enough for humans to pass but present more of a difficulty for bots (Fig. 8.1). They have proved quite effective in validating users, minimizing inappropriate opportunity for anonymity, diminishing the spread of misinformation and harmful content and in general changing incentives for information sharing.

A more sophisticated CAPTCHA-test is the renowned street signs and traffic infrastructure identification (Fig. 8.2). It is no accident that users are asked to identify street signs, from full stops and pedestrian walks over bike paths to highway overpasses and bridges. Google and other companies[17]

Fig. 8.1   A familiar CAPTCHA example

---

[16] Menczer, F. & Hills, T. (2020)." Information Overload Helps Fake News Spread, and Social Media Knows It", *Scientific American*, 01.12.2020, verified 25.05.2021: https://www.scientificamerican.com/article/information-overload-helps-fake-news-spread-and-social-media-knows-it/

[17] O'Malley. J. (2018). "Captcha if you can: how you've been training AI for years without realising it", *Techradar*, 12.01.2018, verified 06.01.2022: https://www.techradar.com/news/captcha-if-you-can-how-youve-been-training-ai-for-years-without-realising-it

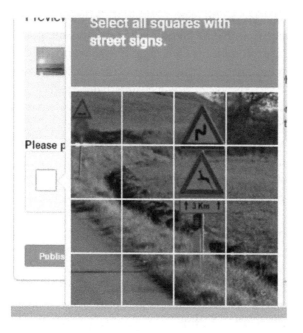

Fig. 8.2 CAPTCHAs as street signs and traffic infrastructure identification tests

using these sorts of CAPTCHAs long ago worked out how to cannibalize and capitalize on the gateways designed to sort human users from bots: the answers provided are useful machine learning data sets to train artificial intelligence, which later may find its way into completely automated cars, drones and other vehicles.

A friction strategy that may stimulate reflection and circumspection among users of some platform service may be actuated by a CAPTCHA-like initiative: give users randomly repeated micro-exams (e.g. multiple choice) when they are about to log in, share, quote, upvote etc. on social media—*but with questions pertaining to the governing community standards of the platform in question.* Such arbitrarily recurring tests may act as bulwarks against information vandalism, hate speech, misinformation, digital harassment, harmful content, exploitation of immaterial rights and all the other items mentioned in platforms' very own community standards. As gateways, they may ensure that users have read and understood—or at least reflected on—what they have agreed to by having a social media profile. Once users familiarize themselves with these standards, it should ease the platform's own burden of enforcing them.

However, they may possibly also change the platforms own behavior and encourage them to:

- Enforce their own adopted principles of content moderation consistently
- Create transparency in their practice
- Stimulate the public debate and political conversation pertaining to the online public sphere, democratic ambition, freedom of expression, privacy, user rights, product declaration and labeling of information products, all themes that the tech giants themselves routinely demand paying increasing attention to.

Here is a concrete blueprint for how governments, politicians, lawmakers and global NGOs interested in CAPTCHA-approach may move forward (Hendricks 2021):

1. Ask the platform the rhetorical question whether they agree it would be beneficial for all parties—themselves, their users, society more broadly—to be reasonably well-versed in their community standards. To avoid another Frances Haugen-moment, chances are that the platform would (or should) agree.
2. Ask the platform to install a friction strategy (that is, not for every single action), such that when users log on, are about to share a post, upvote a post etc. they are, at arbi-

trary times, asked three to five randomly generated questions pertaining to the relevant community standards.

3. If the user can answer, they may immediately proceed to their profile, take the desired action and go about their business.

4. If not, the users have to study the standards in order to answer the questions correctly, after which they may proceed.

It should be easy for the governing body of lawmakers, NGO representatives and other relevant parties to check whether the platform and its other services and apps have implemented and are maintaining the friction strategy in force. By way of example, members of government—read politicians—would likely be set the task of answering these very queries themselves at arbitrary times.

The working hypothesis is that such a friction strategy may actually work in terms of reducing misinformation, hate speech etc. The price to pay for platforms apparently enforcing their own community standards and administering their terms of use among users accordingly is that engagement and data harvest would be reduced, along with their profits.[18] On the other hand, the significant resources they spend on content moderation—and possible legal sanctions and fines for not removing illegal content in time—may make up for these losses and lower advertising sales.

Such a friction strategy based on the social platforms' own community standards would further harness their self-proclaimed *logos, ethos, pathos* and service *raison d'etre* to "bring the world closer together" as Meta/Facebook for instance

---

[18] Edelman, G. (2020). "Stop Saying Facebook Is 'Too Big to Moderate'", *Wired*, 28.07.2020, verified 06.01.2021: https://www.wired.com/story/stop-saying-facebook-too-big-to-moderate/

proclaims.[19] Hence, it should be a win-win for everybody playing ball on the courts of the BigTech—at their own game and by the standards with which they rule the digital public square.

Many NGO's and tech companies have parts to play in the institutional mobilization and so do public education and research institutions—as was the case in the past. In 1929 a group of scientists and scholars—comprised of philosophers, physicists, mathematicians, political scientists and others—wrote an enlightenment manifesto with the somewhat demonstrative title: *Wissenschaftliche Weltauffassung: Der Wiener Kreis*, or *The Scientific Conception of the World: The Vienna Circle*. They met in Vienna's cafés with the initial ambition of making philosophy scientific. They later went on to develop larger and wilder ambitions: a greater ideological and societal difference was now to be made with the help of logic, science, enlightenment and common sense:

> We witness the spirit of the scientific world-conception penetrating in growing measure the forms of personal and public life, in education, upbringing, architecture, and the shaping of economic and social life according to rational principles. *The scientific world-conception serves life, and life receives it.*[20]

Now, a hundred years later, yet another manifesto was written in Vienna, namely the *Vienna Manifesto on Digital Humanism*. The new Vienna manifesto on digital humanism is written by university and sector research employees and research foundation delegates from around the world, in

---

[19] Constine, J. (2017). "Facebook changes mission statement to 'bring the world closer together'", *TechCrunch*, 02.06.2017, verified 14.01.2022: https://techcrunch.com/2017/06/22/bring-the-world-closer-together

[20] Hahn, H., Neurath, O., Carnap, R. (1929). "Wissenschaftliche Weltauffassung: Der Wiener Kreis", reprinted in *Empiricism and Sociology*: 299–318, 1973: https://link.springer.com/chapter/10.1007/978-94-010-2525-6_9

order to fix digital technologies up with a responsible, enlightened and socially beneficial direction resting on the human condition:

> Digital technologies are disrupting societies and questioning our understanding of what it means to be human. The stakes are high and the challenge of building a just and democratic society with humans at the center of technological progress needs to be addressed with determination as well as scientific ingenuity. Technological innovation demands social innovation, and social innovation requires broad societal engagement. (…) We encourage our academic communities, as well as industrial leaders, politicians, policy makers, and professional societies all around the globe, to actively participate in policy formation.[21]

The core principles of the Vienna Manifesto are central for a pervasive mobilization in the information age, particularly the following eight principles:

1. **Digital technologies should be designed to promote democracy and inclusion.**
2. **Privacy and freedom of expression are essential values for democracy and should be at the center of our activities.** Tech platforms need to ensure these values are secured.
3. **Effective regulations, rules and laws, based on a broad public discourse, must be established.** This ensures precision, fairness, equality, transparency and checks-and-balances on platforms, software and algorithms.
4. **Regulators need to invoke anti-trust to break tech monopolies.** Politicians cannot leave all decisions to mar-

---

[21] DIGHUM (2019). *Vienna Manifesto on Digital Humanism,* 19.05.2021, verified 25.05.2021: https://dighum.ec.tuwien.ac.at/dighum-manifesto/

kets or BigTech will concentrate their market power and stifle innovation.

5. **Decisions with consequences that have the potential to affect individual or collective human rights must continue to be made by humans.** Decisions must not be made by automated systems that operate independently of human decision-making competencies and responsibilities.

6. **Academics as well as industrial researchers, must exhibit scientific social responsibility when developing new technologies.** Researchers must collaborate across disciplines, be openly engaged with society and reflect upon their research agenda and approach.

7. **A vision for new interdisciplinary educational curricula must be developed.** The new curricula will pool knowledge from the humanities, social sciences and technology studies and bring an anthropogenic focus while educating the engineers, programmers, etc., of the future.

8. **Practitioners everywhere ought to acknowledge their shared responsibility for the impact of information technologies.** It is essential to understand that technologies are not neutral, as well as reflect upon the potentials and consequences of using technology.

These principles may create a solid foundation for more concrete political initiatives and a greater ideological mobilization.

8.5   Ideological Mobilization

In every new market and with the introduction of a new economy, certain structural problems often emerge with potential as well as real 'collateral damage' to follow. This also applies to the information market ruled by the attention

Fig. 8.3 A meme on "collateral damage" (with inspiration from the wise Jedi Master Yoda from George Lucas' epic *Star Wars*-franchise)

economy (Fig. 8.3). The danger that we as humans wind up as 'collateral damage' is tied to the structural problems.

Structural problem A: People's attention is capitalized, not as a cognitive resource, but as a valuable data asset tuned for surveillance capitalism's business model. The users are the product and BigTech benefits the more we're online, where humans are being auctioned off in the attention economy. Attention is transformed from cognitive resource to capital asset with possibly humans as the collateral damage.

Structural problem B: Connected to the former, and so far borne by a particularly sincere belief in market fundamentalism and what constitutes growth in the information market. This idea is duly reflected in three interconnected theses:

1. Agents in the free information market are self-interested and utility maximizing.
2. Growth may be measured in (allocation of attention and) data-harvest.
3. The purpose of tech platforms is to stimulate (1) and (2).

Given that attention is capitalized and cannibalized in the first structural problem (**A**), it becomes inherently important to *speculate* in what kind of information, independently of high or low quality, users are willing to spend their precious attention on. The information market is not an efficient market where high-quality information survives and poor-quality information is gradually weeded out in the liquid market of information, idea and opinion exchanges. Subprime information products can lead to attention bubbles (Hendricks 2016, 2020; Hendricks and Vestergaard 2018) if growth alone is measured in (allocation of attention and) data-harvest. Misinformation products are the emergent effects (and defects) of a self-interested and profit-maximizing attention allocation market.

Paired with the Matthew effect, both structural problems **A** and **B**, implies on a *microscopic* level, that some voices are heard disproportionately more than others. The uneven distribution of attention generated by accumulated advantages is exacerbated in the same way as increasing financial inequality—and along with it all the unfortunate derivative effects like poverty, marginalization, polarization, rivalry, stigmatization, deprivation and other (self-)defeating deficiencies. Since attention is both a cognitive resource and a capital asset, a straight line may be drawn from its cognitive to pecuniary value.

Macroscopically it comes to light that those who are able to receive a lot of attention also hold the power of information (and determine what when and how much information should be made available to whom, when, where and how). The information borne infrastructure benefits from the Matthew effect, where more breeds more. The more one controls the quantity (as well as quality) of the circulating information products and global attention allocation the more one receives in return. This entails that global market dominance, monopolies, and gigantic monetary wealth are concentrated in the hands of very few tech companies in the information market.

And this is how we wound up here. The pressing question now is how we ideologically curb the capitalized information market and come up with the political initiatives needed to address the two structural problems.

Politicians, in the EU and US especially, have recently begun to consider, on an ideological plane, the core principles of the Vienna manifesto. Mobilization differs a bit depending on which side of the Atlantic ocean it happens. Broadly speaking, the EU has initially focused on addressing structural problem **A** but has also moved on to deal with **B**, while the US has devoted special attention to **B**.

A 2019 survey of EU's citizens revealed that 74% of the respondents want to know more about how social platforms utilize their data.[22] A year prior to the survey, the EU had adopted the European data protection law (GDPR), as a regulatory measure against the tech industry and to address structural problem **A**. GDPR gives citizens and users more authority over how companies may use their data. The legislation has served as inspiration for proposals in Brazil for example, and while the US does not yet have federal data-protection laws, California has personal data protection rules reminiscent of GDPR.[23]

In order to deal with structural problem **B**, the EU is ratifying "The Digital Services Act" and "Digital Markets Act". This legislative package, developed by Margrethe Vestager, a well-known Danish parliamentarian with the telling title

---

[22] Data.europa.eu (2019). "Special Eurobarometer 503: Attitudes towards the impact of digitalization on daily lives", Directorate-General for Communication, verified 27.05.2021: https://data.europa.eu/data/datasets/s2228_92_4_503_eng?locale=en

[23] Hopelhorn, S. (2020). "California Consumer Privacy Act (CCPA) vs. GDPR", *Varonis*, 17.06.2020, verified 01.07.2021: https://www.varonis.com/blog/ccpa-vs-gdpr/

"Executive Vice President of the European Commission for A Europe Fit for the Digital Age", was presented to the European Parliament and European Council in December 2020. The legislation is an attempt to force BigTech to take responsibility for the content on their platforms, to become transparent about their business models and their editorial and algorithmic data curation practices. Simultaneously the laws will help stimulate level playing fields and fair competition in the information marketplace or as Margrethe Vestager noted in her speech to the EU-commission of October 2020:

> The new rules will also require digital services — especially the biggest platforms — to be open about the way they shape the digital world that we see. They'll have to report on what they've done to take down illegal material. They'll have to tell us how they decide what information and products to recommend to us, and which ones to hide —and give us the ability to influence those decisions, instead of simply having them made for us. And they'll have to tell us who's paying for the ads that we see, and why we've been targeted by a certain ad.[24]

Renowned American historian Francis Fukuyama recently joined the discussion with an initiative that is both institutional and ideological:

> We need trustworthy organizations that can gain access and edit the content that we see e.g. on Facebook and Google. I call it "middleware" — a program that has full-access to the behind-the-scenes data of BigTech and which can ensure that we users are given more control over our news and data.

---

[24] Vestager, M. (2020). "Building Trust in Technology", *EPC Webinar*, Digital Clearinghouse, 29 October 2020, verified 27.05.2021: https://ec.europa.eu/commission/commissioners/2019-2024/vestager/announcements/speech-executive-vice-president-margrethe-vestager-building-trust-technology_en

Otherwise, the current dominance that is secured via opaque algorithms will only increase.[25]

The EU had previously addressed the opaque and competition distorting algorithms employed by BigTech to gain market dominance. In 2017, for example, the EU commission fined Google 2.4 billion euros for favoring their own comparison shopping service.

Even after Google made changes, in response to the ruling, it still only allowed less than 1% of the traffic to be routed to rival comparison shopping portals.[26] Facebook joined the ranks of Google, when the EU, in the spring of 2021, launched a formal investigation into how the company's advertising data is used to compete against the platform's advertisers in the classified ads market.[27] Similarly, Amazon received a 888 million euro fine in 2021 for GDPR violations.[28] The EU-commission continuously try to reach out to the Irish government to collect 13 billion euros in back taxes from Apple, hinting that BigTech can look forward to a more tight knit EU tax-regulation. The EU's next move is to map whether it is possible to regulate the use of artificial intelligence in the tech industry.

---

[25] Trads, D. (2021)." Francis Fukuyama tordner mod tech-giganternes magt", *Jyllandsposten*, 27.05.2021, verified 29.05.2021: https://jyllands-posten.dk/international/europa/ECE13005995/francis-fukuyama-tordner-mod-techgiganternes-magt/

[26] Espinoza, J. (2020). "Google Shopping accused of failing to address competition problems", *Financial Times*, 28.09.2020, verified 27.05.2021: https://www.ft.com/content/4c6f06b9-a984-429e-b397-332a1779bd71

[27] White, A. (2021). "Facebook Data Trove Probed as Europe Turns Screw on Big Tech (1)", *Bloomberg Law*, 04.06.2021, verified 14.06.2021: https://news.bloomberglaw.com/tech-and-telecom-law/facebook-is-vestagers-next-big-tech-target-as-eu-opens-probe

[28] Bodoni, S. (2021). "Amazon Gets Record $888 Million EU Fine Over Data Violations", *Bloomberg News*, 30.07.2021, verified 13.08.2021: https://www.bloomberg.com/news/articles/2021-07-30/amazon-given-record-888-million-eu-fine-for-data-privacy-breach

Huge battles lay ahead, or as Vestager said about the new laws (Fig. 8.4):

> But perhaps the biggest challenge we face with enforcement is making sure that we have the right legal framework and powers to keep digital markets competitive and fair.[29]

One complex predicament is worth noting: As long as we ideologically and legislatively accept surveillance capitalism's business model in liberal democracies, without any real constraints on how, how much and way in which attention is allocated and data is harvested, it will be difficult to redeem any effective control. Note, that the official argument for harvesting, segmenting and selling massive amounts of data is that it enhances UX—User Experience.[30] As long as "enhanced user experience" remains central, the illusion that

Fig. 8.4 A tweet from Margrethe Vestager while working on the "Digital Services Act" and "Digital Markets Act", October 30, 2020

---

[29] Amaro, S. (2020)." The EU is about to announce new rules for Big Tech — and there's not much they can do about it", CNBC, 05.11.2020, verified 27.05.2021: $https://www.cnbc.com/2020/11/05/digital-services-act-how-the-eu-is-going-after-big-tech.html

[30] Singh, A. (2019). *Big Data Analytics for Improved Accuracy, Efficiency, and Decision Making in Digital Design*. Advances in Marketing, Customer Relationship, Management and E-services. (AMCRMES) Book Series.

data is harvested to benefit users will continue to be perpetuated. Add to this, that the purpose of data harvest is to refine the recommendation systems of algorithms in such a way that users increasingly get precisely what their interests dictate, from hula-hoops and hamster wheels to political products. In total, the business model of tech platforms is strengthened continually through a one-way self-reinforcing feedback mechanism, all the way down to user level. Amplified data-harvest and segmentation improves user experience through algorithmic recommendation systems that boost data harvest, -segmentation and -sales (or -leasing), which in turn cements the necessity of surveillance while continuously reinforcing information power as the revenue of BigTech (Fig. 8.5).

The current business models of tech platforms and their recommendation-based feedback mechanisms stoke division, stimulate polarization and echo-chamber effects (Brugnoli et al. 2019), (Cinelli et al. 2021) that are not necessarily conducive to the kind of democratic dialogue that the ideological principles and legislative actions, that have been put forward, seek to stimulate as whistleblower Frances Haugen has also argued. Unless there is political will to look at whether surveillance capitalism's data driven feedback model should be limited directly or deemed principally illegal in practice, it will remain immensely complicated to fully honor the ambitions of the EU to address structural problems **A** and **B** and the aspirations of Americans to do the same.

While Europe attempts to tackle structural problems **A** and **B** through policy and legislation, Americans have initially and increasingly focused their attention on the market dominance of BigTech. A couple of reasons for this difference in focus is interestingly tied to prior legislative practices and traditions in the US.

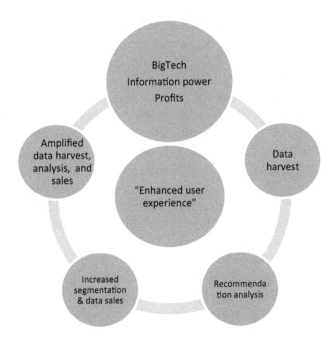

Fig. 8.5 "Enhanced user experience" at the center of a self-reinforcing feedback for amplified data harvest and algorithmic recommendation systems, that strengthen the information power and revenue of BigTech in a (yet) never ending loop

In 1996 the US Congress passed some of the first legislation dealing with the Internet, but as it turned out the legislation worked overwhelmingly to the advantage of the tech industry. Legislative amendment Section §230 of the Communications Decency Act was initially thought to secure and strengthen freedom of expression and online innovation by granting internet service providers, hosting or reproducing speech and text, with immunity. Otherwise they would likely risk being subject to legislation that would hold them legally accountable for what is said and done on their sites.

> No provider or user of an interactive computer service shall
> be treated as the publisher or speaker of any information
> provided by another information content provider. (47
> U.S.C. § 230)[31]

This immunity from legal accountability not only applies to
what are labelled regular service providers, but also to a broad
array of "interactive computer service providers", which basically includes any online-service that publishes third party
material.

There are exceptions when it comes to certain criminal
acts and for copyrights but otherwise there is full protection
for those who publish or share third party material online.
Section 230 is supplemented by section §230(c)(2) that
establishes a kind of 'Good Samaritan' protection against
civil lawsuits aimed at Internet service providers and interactive service portals when it comes to the removal or moderation of third party content that providers may find obscene
or offensive—and this even applies to statements protected
by the Constitution—as long as it is done in good faith. In
practice §230 left the tech industry, with BigTech at the
helm, free of accountability for basically all third party material on their portals and websites since the mid-1990s and up
until now … but new voices have begun to gather steam in
Washington.

After the 2016 and 2020 US presidential election misinformation campaigns; the Capitol insurrection on January
6th 2021, the following Deplatforming Day on January 7th
2021, *The Facebook Files* and a political system that since has
become the wiser as to what BigTech actually is (an alarmingly absent knowledge until around the so-called *Techlash* in

---

[31] §230. Protection for private blocking and screening of offensive material, Text
contains those laws in effect on May 28, 2021, verified 29.05.2021: ttps://uscode.
house.gov/view.xhtml?req=(title:47 section:230 edition:prelim)

2018, i.e., the scandalously uninformed "Senator, we run ads" hearing), their business models, product portfolio and information market dominance, the views of US politicians and legislators on Section §230 has begun to change. Republicans and Democrats alike, now understand that BigTech have come to represent an important part of the critical information borne infrastructure and that the public space to some extent has been transferred to private enterprise. So, Republicans have suggested a reform of §230 to remove the legislative shield that protects tech platforms from the responsibility of third party material and user posts. More specifically the suggestions are:

- Tech platforms' sovereign control over excluding users on the basis of their views or political positions must be limited.
- Tech platforms must be subject to a "fair content moderation practice" that secures and deals with illegal content such as selling drugs or child abuse.
- Tech platforms must limit content moderation practices to certain types of statements that are not protected by the First Amendment.
- Tech platforms' protections in decisions regarding discriminatory content moderation based on (political) standpoints must be removed.[32]

For example, under a law ratified under Florida governor Ron DeSantis—the first of its kind—and with reference to the violation of citizens' rights to free speech, tech platforms are forbidden to "deplatform" users permanently. Tech platforms that do not comply with this legislation stand to

---

[32] Feiner, L. (2021). "House Republican staff outline principles to reform tech's liability shield", *CNBC*, 15.04.2021: https://www.cnbc.com/2021/04/15/house-republicans-outline-principles-for-reforming-section-230.html

receive daily fines of up to $250,000 until a repeal of user sanction is met.[33] Protecting freedom of expression was originally one of the main reasons for adopting §230, but it has reached a point, as prominent Republican senator Lindsey Graham suggests, where §230 either needs to be rewritten or removed to safeguard free speech via legislation and potential lawsuits: "I'm more determined than ever to strip Section 230 from BigTech (Twitter) that let them be immune from lawsuits."[34]

Democrats have proposed similar changes to §230 in the so-called SAFE TECH Act, in early 2021. Here they suggest, among other things, a veritable changing of words in §230, so that the word 'information' is replaced by 'speech' as in "No provider or user of an interactive computer service shall be treated as the publisher or speaker of any *speech* provided by another information content provider." The change is meant to limit the scope of the law and potentially remove the liability protections of tech platforms for the undercurrent of other illegal online information sharing practices. Included in part of the SAFE TECH package is a piece of legislation, the purpose of which is to target advertising and paid content and potentially hold tech platforms accountable for the damaging content they profit from. It is meant to keep tech platforms from highlighting misinformation and fake news, while making it clear that they can be held accountable, as providers of broadband, for advertisements that for instance violate civil rights statutes. Overhauling §230 is urgently needed as one of the bill's proponents, Democratic senator Mike Warner expressed:

---

[33] Ingram, D. (2021)." Florida governor signs ban on 'deplatforming' by tech companies", *NBC News*, 25.05.2021, verified 29.05.2021: https://www.nbcnews.com/news/amp/rcna1018

[34] Graham, L. (2021). Tweet, Twitter, 09.01.2021, verified 25.06.2021: https://twitter.com/lindseygrahamsc/status/1347713461246169089?lang=en

"Section 230 has provided a 'Get Out of Jail Free' card to the largest platform companies even as their sites are used by scam artists, harassers and violent extremists to cause damage and injury," (…) "This bill doesn't interfere with free speech — it's about allowing these platforms to finally be held accountable for harmful, often criminal behavior enabled by their platforms to which they have turned a blind eye for too long."[35]

While it may well be that Republicans and Democrats have very different motives for reforming Section 230 and other initiatives that limit BigTech, one thing they do agree on is that the tech industry has been held unaccountable for too long and grown to become behemoths—and the *Facebook Files* of WSJ and Frances Haugen's testimony in 2021 only bolstered their joint convictions.

8.6   Size Matters

The US has a strong political tradition for politicians to strike back when private enterprise creates monopoly-like conditions in markets. Through time large companies such as AT&T, Standard Oil, Kodak and Microsoft have been exposed to US antitrust laws. Too great a concentration of power stifles innovation, competition, initiative and vigor on the free market. It is not good for consumers and it slows the market as an engine of long term growth and prosperity.

For decades, nonetheless, the so-called *Chicago School of Political Economists*[36] succeeded in convincing legislators and

---

[35] Birnbaum, E. & Lapowsky, I. (2021)." This is the Democrats' plan to limit Section 230", *Protocol*, 05.02.2021, verified 29.05.2021: https://www.protocol.com/policy/democrats-plan-section-230

[36] The Chicago School of Political Economy (1975). "Introduction", *Journal of Economic Issues*, Vol IX, No.4: 585–604.

the executive branch of government of a very narrow reading of antitrust measures to be used solely when 'consumer welfare' is threatened.[37] Legislators and courts should only punish monopolies that raise consumer prices which came to be known as the consumer-welfare standard (Wu 2018). In practice this means that the legislation has barely been used over the past many years—it also seems a bit outdated considering that many tech platforms offer their services for 'free'.

But the winds in Washington are now blowing in a more fist clenching activistic bi-partisan direction of a Brandaisian nature. The reference is to Louis Brandeis, a nineteenth Century legal scholar and Supreme Court Justice, arguing that individuals or corporations amassing too much power could exert pressure on political systems. In such cases governments have a duty to intervene breaking up such entities to ensure competitive markets: "Antimonopolism is the extension of the basic concept of checks and balances into the political economy" as Barry Lynn, founder of the Open Markets think tank, has noted.[38] This line of reasoning is not anti-business and detrimental to the basic idea of free markets as Chair of the Federal Trade Committee, Lina Khan (who in 2020 again put forth a sweeping antitrust suit against Meta/Facebook pertaining to the compnay's earlier acquisition of Instagram and WhatsApp) rehearsed in an interview:

> I think anti-trust and anti-monopoly and fair competition are enormously pro-business. Monopolistic business practices are not conducive to a robust and striving economy.[39]

---

[37] Drivas, I. (2019). "Reassessing the Chicago School of Anti-trust Law", University of Chicago, Law, 04.06.2019, verified 29.05.2021: https://www.law.uchicago.edu/news/reassessing-chicago-school-antitrust-law

[38] Kolhatkar, S. (2021). "The Enforcer: Lina Khan's battle to rein in Big Tech", *The New Yorker*, December 6: 48–58.

[39] Kolhatkar, S. (2021). "The Enforcer: Lina Khan's battle to rein in Big Tech", *The New Yorker*, December 6: 48–58.

Worries have thus resurfaced also at the political level about the sheer size, financial concentration of power, co-opting of the public space and critical information infrastructure as well as the homegrown guidelines of BigTech, have currently given rise to broader and more ambitious societal and democratic means of interpreting antitrust legislation.[40] The time has come to rehabilitate antitrust laws. At the July 2020 BigTech AntiTrust Hearing, Republican Chairman David N. Cicillin made the following remark in his opening statement—in the remote (online) presence of Jeff Bezos (Amazon), Sundar Pichai (Alphabet), Tim Cook (Apple) and Mark Zuckerberg (Meta/Facebook):

> Open markets are predicated on the idea that, if a company harms people, consumers, workers, and business partners will chose another option. That choice is no longer possible. Concentrated economic power leads to concentrated political power. This investigation goes to the heart of whether we as a people govern ourselves, or let ourselves be governed by private monopolies.[41]

Jim Banks, leader of the Republican Study Committee in the House of Representatives, later chimed in and wrote the following on Twitter on May 5th 2021 pertaining to the concentration of the pollical power of BigTech:

> If Facebook is so big it thinks it can silence the leaders you elect, it's time for conservatives to pursue an antitrust agenda.[42]

---

[40] Edgerton, A. (2021)." All-Night Antitrust Debate Moves Big Tech Bills Forward (3)", *Bloomberg Law*, 24.06.2021, verified 25.06.2021: https://news.bloomberglaw.com/antitrust/all-night-antitrust-debate-moves-big-tech-legislation-forward

[41] Cicilline, D.N. (2020) "Cicilline Opening Statement at BigTech Antitrust Hearing", 29.07.2020, verified 23.01.2022: https://cicilline.house.gov/press-release/cicilline-opening-statement-big-tech-antitrust-hearing

[42] Banks, J. (2021). Tweet, Twitter 05.05.2021, verified 16.06.2021: https://twitter.com/RepJimBanks/status/1389942124406198277?ref_src=twsrc%5Etfw

Republicans, in a remarkable u-turn considering past track record, have now coupled freedom of expression (traditionally conceived as an ideological flagship in the free marketplace of ideas) with competition law (traditionally viewed as a financial flagship to secure fair and balanced competition in the market for goods and services). It is a connection that many Republicans simultaneously yet may feel somewhat uneasy about. As Reagan-era Republican luminary Mark Fowler admitted with some reservation:

> We may not like it as Republicans — I don't. (…) But I like more the idea of free markets, with free marketplaces of ideas. And that really is the higher value. That is really what Republicans are missing in all this.[43]

Viewed in this light and point in time, where information in the attention economy has gained a pecuniary value—freedom of expression and antitrust are really the same side of the coin. Free speech becomes a democratic" product" subject to competition—and may come under pressure—in an information market that in the final analysis is controlled by the interests of the attention economy. From this vantage point it is not far from the proposal that the free marketplace of ideas and goods may—or should—be regulated with the same sort of interventions.

If this happens, it is, under any circumstance, an admission that market forces, in an era where information has attained value not just in form of enlightenment but also in dollars and cents, also apply to the free marketplace of ideas and the democratic stage. But according to the pillars of democracy, on which our Western liberal democracies are

---

[43] Hendel, J. (2021). "How Trump's fights with tech transformed Republicans' beliefs on free speech", *Politico*, 18.01.2021, verified 29.05.2021: https://www.politico.com/news/2021/01/18/trump-free-speech-big-tech-459833

modeled, no one should have privileged access or status as a result of financial advantage or large market shares. Nonetheless, "follow the money" nowadays seems to also apply to democratic values such as freedom of expression. So where would this development lead us as a (global) society?

8.7   The Ministry of Truth

One scenario is that nation states and supranational bodies simply give up and leave societal development and state administration to the private and global tech industry's entrepreneurship and control. A *corporatocracy*, where monumental tech businesses control everything from democracy to finances and fix the frame, form and fixture of people's lives, self-determination, autonomy and authority. It would not bode well for democracy and the authority of people if the rule of citizens and their autonomy becomes a function of private business interests and annual business reporting. Nor do BigTech companies seem to be interested in taking on this responsibility. As expressed by Zuckerberg during the 2019 Senate hearing, safeguarding democracy is "above our pay grade".[44]

Another scenario has at its core what might immediately appear to be a more democratic leaning: Values such as freedom of expression, assembly, religion and other democratic instilled privileges are still governed by tools of the trade gathered from the fiscal policy toolbox. Income and resource allocation measures, efficiency and economic stabilization measures become means by which to control both the

---

[44] Lutz, E. (2019). "Zuckerberg Says Safeguarding Democracy Is "Above Our Pay Grade"", *Vanity Fair*, 27.06.2019, verifceret 05.07.2021: https://www.vanityfair.com/news/2019/06/zuckerberg-says-safeguarding-democracy-is-above-our-pay-grade-aspen-ideas

economy and collective spirit of society. It will provide a new legitimacy for establishing a dedicated "Ministry of Truth" in the government administration. Not as Orwell's ministry, which at its outset is a propaganda ministry, that both falsifies historical events and defines truth. But more accurately, a ministry that continually monitors the flow of money in the new online public sphere and that intervenes with fiscal tools if necessary. This may prove especially pertinent if it turns out that the public sphere and the public debate in it may be hijacked, manipulated and twisted sowing division and hatred by secret apps, like Tek Fog, as recent reporting seems to indicate.[45]

The Ministry of Truth would then, with its democratic statutory power, decide where citizens and users direct their attention, what data can be harvested, analyzed and sold, and how large of a market share, of the combined free idea- and financial markets, that privately owned tech businesses should be allowed to own, before selling out democratic values. *A democratically concocted Ministry of Truth, based on surveillance capitalism and designed to fit an information market governed by an attention economy.*

This fact alone, that a state can decide or exert direct influence on where citizens can or should direct their attention and what data may be harvested and by whom, is not immediately compatible with the democratically secured rights of personal freedom. Where and how attention is allocated within the realm of the already adopted legislation, is the sole domain of citizens and users alike. Even with a new and fanciful *raison d'être* for merging the markets of ideas and financial products into one, the state should not have a Ministry of Truth. Nor should BigTech be left alone with the task

---

[45] Kaul, A. & Kumar, D. (2022)." Tek Fog: An App With BJP Footprints for Cyber Troops to Automate Hate, Manipulate Trends, *The Wire*, 06.01.2022, verified 07.01.2022: https://thewire.in/tekfog/en/1.html

since it may lead to the aforementioned corporatocratic scenario. None of the two scenarios can be defended democratically, nor are they viable.

Free exchanges of opinions must not be made subject to the freedom of market mobility, as they will then have lost their freedom. The idea of putting public space in private hands is just as irreconcilable as a liberal democracy is with a Ministry of Truth. There will only be one loser—us. It may well be that too little has been done in past decades but better late than never ... *The roaring 2020s* is the time to mobilize individually, institutionally and ideologically to create a sustainable Internet and robust democracy—not version 2.0—but a lasting version with staying power.

References

Alter, A. (2017). *Irresistible: Why we can't stop checking, scrolling, clicking and watching*. New York: Penguin Press, s.13-89.

Aral, S. (2020). *The Hype Machine: How Social Media Disrupts Our Elections, Our Economy, and Our Health — And How We Must Adapt*. Cambridge: MIT Press.

Aronson, E., Wilson, T. D., *Akert, R. D. & Sommers, S. R. (2015)*. Social psychology *(9th, illustrated, revised ed.). London:* Pearson Education.

Barberis, N. C. (2013). "Thirty years of prospect theory in economics: A review and assessment." *Journal of Economic Perspectives, 27*(1), 173-96.

Bartle, R. (1996). "Hearts, clubs, diamonds, spades: Players who suit MUDs", *Journal of Mud Research*, 1996.

Bastick, Z. (2021). "Would you notice if fake news changed your behavior? An experiment on the unconscious effects of disinformation," *Computers in Human Behavior*, Volume 116.

Baumgartner, F.R., Jones, B.D. & Mortensen, P.B. (2014). "Punctuated Equilibrium Theory: Explaining Stability and

© The Author(s), under exclusive license to Springer Nature Switzerland AG 2022
V. F. Hendricks, C. Mehlsen, *The Ministry of Truth*,
https://doi.org/10.1007/978-3-030-98629-2

Change in Public Policy", in *Theory of the Policy Processes*, Weible, C.M. & Sabatier, P.A. (red.). Boulder, CO: Westview Press: 59-103.

Berger, J. (2013). *Contagious*. New York: Simon & Schuster.

Berger, Jonah A. and Milkman, Katherine L. (2009). "What Makes Online Content Viral?" SSRN 25.

Brady, W.J., Wills, J.A., Jost, J.T., Tucker, J.A., Bavel, J.V.J. (2017). "Moral contagion in social networks", *Proceedings of the National Academy of Sciences*, July 2017, 114 (28) 713-731.

Brashier, N.M. & Marsh, J. (2020). "Judging Truth", *Annual Review of Psychology* 2020 71:1, 499-515.

Brugnoli, E., Cinelli, M., Quattrociocchi, W. *et al.* (2019). "Recursive patterns in online echo chambers," *Nature, Sci Rep* **9,** 20118 (2019). https://doi.org/10.1038/s41598-019-56191-7

Chafkin, M. (2021). *The Contrarian: Peter Thiel and Silicon Valley's Pursuit of Power*. New York: Penguin Press.

Ciampaglia, G.L., Nematzadeh, A., Menczer, F. et al. (2018). "How algorithmic popularity bias hinders or promotes quality," *Sci Rep* **8,** 15951.

Cinelli, M., Gianmarco, F.M.D, Galeazzi, A, Quattrociocchi, W. & Starnini, m. (2021). "The echo chamber effect on social media", *Proceedings of the National Academy of Sciences*, March, 118 (9) e2023301118; DOI: https://doi.org/10.1073/pnas.2023301118

Conover, M.D., Gonçalves, B., Flammini, A. et al. (2012). "Partisan asymmetries in online political activity." *EPJ Data Sci.* **1,** 6 (2012). https://doi.org/10.1140/epjds6.

Eyal, N. (2014). *Hooked: How to Build Habit-Forming Products*. New York: Random House.

Eyal, Nir (2019). *Indistractable: How to Control Your Attention and Choose Your Life*. New York: BenBella Books.

Fogg, B. J. (2002). *Persuasive Technology: Using Computers to Change What We Think and Do*. New York: Morgan Kaufman.

Foucault, M. (1979). *Discipline and punish: The birth of the prison*. New York: Vintage Books.

Franck, G. (1999). "The Economy of Attention", *Telepolis* 7, December.

Franck G. (2002): "The scientific economy of attention: A novel approach to the collective rationality of science". *Scientometrics* 55(1), 3–26

Franck, G. (2016). "Vanity Fairs: Competition in the Service of Self-Esteem", *Mind & Matter* Vol. 14(2), pp. 155–165.

Franck G. (2016a). "The economy of attention in the age of neo-liberalism", *Communication in the Era of Attention Scarcity*, ed. by C. Roda. Heidelberg: Springer.

Franck, G. (2019). "The economy of attention". *Journal of Sociology*, 55(1), 8–19.

Frankfurt, H. (1986). *On Bullshit*. Princeton: Princeton University Press.

Glenski, M. & Weninger, T. (2017). "Rating Effects on Social News Posts and Comments," *ACM Transactions on Intelligent Systems and Technology*, article 78: https://doi.org/10.1145/2963104.

Haidt, J. (2012). *The Righteous Mind: Why good people are divided by politics and religion*. New York: Penguin Group.

Hagen, L., Neely, S., Keller, T.E., Scharf, R., & Vasquez, F.E. (2020). "Rise of the Machines? Examining the Influence of Social Bots on a Political Discussion Network," *Social Science Computer Review*. March 2020: 236–256.

Harford, T. (2020). *How to Make the World Add Up: Ten Rules for Thinking Differently About Numbers*. New York: The Bridge Street Press.

Hendricks, V.F. (2006). *Mainstream and Formal Epistemology*. New York: Cambridge University Press.

Hendricks, V.F. (2016). *Spræng boblen. Sådan bevarer du fornuften i en ufornuftig verden*. København: Gyldendal.

Hendricks, V.F. (2017). "Attention Economics and Fake News/ The ceremonial lecture at The Annual Commemoration 2017 given by professor Vincent F. Hendricks", HippoReads/ Universitetsavisen, 17.11.2017

Hendricks, V. F. (2020). *Vend Verden: Genvind autonomien i en digital tidsalder*. København: Politikens Forlag.

Hendricks, V.F. (2021). "Opmærksomhedsøkonomien i medie-markedet", in *Når medierne sætter dagsordenen*, Borberg, V. et al. (red.). København: Djøf Forlag: 323–342.

Hendricks, V.F. (2021b). "Turning the Tables: Using BigTech community standards as friction strategies", OECD Forum, 20.12.2021, verified 06.01.2022: https://www.oecd-forum.org/posts/turning-the-tables-using-bigtech-community-standards-as-friction-strategies.

Hendricks, V.F. (2022). "Critical (Democratic) Infrastructure and BigTech", OECD Forum, 01.02.2022, verified 24.04.2022: https://www.oecd-forum.org/posts/critical-democratic-infrastructure-and-bigtech.

Hendricks, V.F. & Hansen, P.G. (2011). *Oplysningens blinde vinkler: En åndselitær kritik af informationssamfundet*. Frederiksberg: Samfundslitteratur.

Hendricks, V.F. & Hansen, P.G. (2016). *Infostorms: Why do we "like". Explaining Individual Behavior on the Social Net*. New York: Copernicus Books/Springer Nature.

Hendricks, V.F. & Stjernfelt, F. (2007). *Tal en tanke: Om klarhed og nonsense i tænkning og kommunikation*. Frederiksberg: Samfundslitteratur.

Hendricks, V.F. & Vestergaard, M. (2018). *Fake News: Når virkeligheden taber*. København: Gyldendal.

Hendricks, V.F. & Vestergaard, M. (2019). *Reality Lost. Markets of Attention, Misinformation and Manipulation*. New York: Springer Nature.

Hendricks, V.F. & Vestergaard, M. (2020). "I opmærksomhedsøkonomien er det indbringende at være kendt for at være kendt", *Berlingske* 24.02.2020.

Humprecht, E. & Esser, F. (2017). "Diversity in Online News: On the Importance of ownership types and media system types. *Journalism Studies*, online first: Pages 1–23 | Published online: 10 Apr 2017.

Huxley, A. (1932). *Brave New World*. Vintage Classics; 1st edition (January 1, 2007)

IDA (2021). "Onlinespil gambler med børns data", published by IDA & Dataethics. Copenhagen

Jagiello, R.D. & Hills, T. (2018). "Bad News Has Wings: Dread Risk Mediates Social Amplification in Risk Communication", *Risk Analysis* 38, 10: 2193-2207.

Jaschke, K. & Ötsch, C. (2003). *Stripping Las Vegas: a Contextual Review of Casino Resort Architecture*. El Verso.

Kahneman, D. & Tversky, A. (1979). "Prospect theory: An analysis of decision under risk." *Econometrica, 47*, 263-291.

Kahneman, D. (2011). *Thinking, fast and slow*. London: Allen Lane.

Klanker, M., Sandberg, T., Joosten, R., Willuhn, I., Feenstra, M. & Denys, D. (2015). "Phasic dopamine release induced by positive feedback predicts individual differences in reversal learning", *Neurobiology of learning and memory, 125*, 135–145.

Lauritzen, A.M. & Stjernfelt, F. (2018). *Your Post has Been Removed*. New York: Springer.

Marker, S.L. & Hendricks, V.F. (2019). *Os og Dem: Identitetspolitiske akser, ideer og afsporede debatter*. København: Gyldendal.

Martel, C., Pennycook, G. & Rand, D.G. (2020). "Reliance on emotion promotes belief in fake news," *Cogn. Research* **5**, 47.

Matt (25). *The New Testament*. BroadStreet Publishing Group LLC; Deluxe edition, 2022.

McNamee, R. (2019). *Zucked: Waking up to the Facebook Catastrophe*. New York: HarperCollins.

Mehlsen, C. (2020). *Homo Futura: 7 kompetencer til en bedre fremtid*. Frederikshavn: Dafolo.

Mehlsen, C. (2020a). *Influencere – de nye unge mediehuse*. Mediernes Forsknings- og Innovationscenter. Syddansk Universitet.

Mehlsen, C. & Hendricks, V.F. (2018). *Hvordan bliver vi digitalt dannede?* København: Informations Forlag.

Mehlsen, C. & Hendricks, V.F. (2019). "Influenceres magt handler om mere end reklame", kronik, Politiken, 09.02.2019.

Mehlsen, C. & Hendricks, V.F. (2019a) (red.). *LIKE: Shitstorme, fake news, fear of missing out. What's not to like?* København: Center for Information og Boblestudier, Københavns Universitet: www.digitaluddannelse.org.

Mehlsen, C. & Hendricks, V.F. (2020). "Sociale medier og selvfortællinger", *KvaN*, 118, December, p. 69-79.

Orwell, G. (1949). *1984*. Signet Classic (January 1, 1961).

Pacheo, D. Hui, P.-M, Torres-Lugo, C et al. (2021). "Uncovering Coordinated Networks on Social Media: Methods and Case

Studies", roc. AAAI Intl. Conference on Web and Social Media (ICWSM) 2021.

Postman, N. (1985). *Amusing Ourselves to Death: Public Discourse in the Age of Show Business*. New York: Penguin Books.

Rogers, R. (2020). "Deplatforming: Following extreme internet celebrities to Telegram and alternative media", *European Journal of Communication* 2020, Vol. 35 (3) 213-229.

Rosling, H. (2018). *Factfulness: Ten Reasons We're Wrong About the World – and Why Things Are Better Than You Think*. New York: Flatiron Books.

Sasahara, K., Chen, W., Peng, H. et al. (2021). "Social influence and unfollowing accelerate the emergence of echo chambers." *J Comput Soc Sc* **4,** 381–402.

Schüll, N.D. (2012). *Addiction by Design: Machine Gambling in Las Vegas*. Princeton: Princeton University Press.

Shao, C., Ciampaglia, G.L., Varol, O. et al.(2018). "The spread of low-credibility content by social bots," *Nat. Commun.* **9,** 4787.

Simon, H. (1955). "A Behavioral Model of Rational Choice", *Quarterly Journal of Economics*, 69(1): 99–118. doi:https://doi.org/10.2307/1884852.

Simon, H. (1957). *Models of Man*, New York: John Wiley.

Simon, H.A. (1971) 'Designing Organizations for an Information-rich World', pp. 37–52 in Greenberger, M. (ed.) *Computers, Communication, and the Public Interest*. Baltimore, MD: Johns Hopkins University Press.

Snowden, E. (2019). *Permanent Record*. New York: Metropolitan Books.

Skinner, B. F. (1938). *The behavior of organisms: An experimental analysis*. Seventh printing (1966). East Norwalk, CT, US: Appleton-Century-Crofts.

Skinner, B. F. (1953). *Science and human behavior*. New York: Macmillan.

Strue Frederiksen, C. & Hendricks, V.F. (2018). *Kæmp for kloden: Når politik, videnskab og erhvervsliv sammen tager ansvar*. København: Gyldendal.

Teixeira, T. S. (2014). "The rising cost of consumer attention: Why should you care, and what you can do about it", *Harvard Business School*, Working Paper 14-055, January 17, 2014.

Unkelbach, C., Koch, A., Silva, R.R. & Garcia-Marques ,T. (2019). "Truth by Repetition: Explanations and Implications," *Current Directions in Psychological Science.* 28(3): 247-253.

Vaccari, C. & Chadwick, A. (2020). "Deepfakes and Disinformation: Exploring the Impact of Synthetic Political Video on Deception, Uncertainty, and Trust in News", *Social Media + Society*, 2020: 1–13.

Vaidhyanathan, S. (2012). *The Googlization of Everything* (And Why We Should Worry), Updated Edition. California: University of California Press.

Vestergaard, M. (2019). *Digital Totalitarisme.* København: Informations Forlag.

Vestergaard, M. (2022). *Markets of Attention, Misinformation and Surveillance: Critical Studies in Digital Capitalism.* PhD Dissertation, Center for Information and Bubble Studies, University of Copenhagen.

Vogel, H.L., (2010): *Financial Markets: Bubbles and Crashes.* New York: Cambridge University Press.

Vosoughi, S., Roy, D. & Aral, S. (2018). "The Spread of True and False News Online", Science, Vol. 359, Issue 6380, pp. 1146-1151.

Webster, J. G. (2014). *The Marketplace of Attention.* Cambridge: The MIT Press.

Wu, T. (2016). *The attention merchants.* New York: Knopf.

Wu, T. (2018). *The Curse of Bigness: Antitrust in the New Gilded Age.* New York: Columbia Global Reports

Yan H.Y., Yang K-C, Menczer F. & Shanahan J. (2020). "Asymmetrical perceptions of partisan political bots," *New Media & Society.* July 2020.

Zuboff, S. (2019). *The Age of Surveillance Capitalism.* New York: Profile Books.

Zuboff S (2019a). "Surveillance Capitalism and the Challenge of Collective Action", *New Labor Forum*, 28(1): 10-29.

CPSIA information can be obtained
at www.ICGtesting.com
Printed in the USA
BVHW010938010722
641020BV00023B/482